# Camino Notes

WALKING THE WAY WITH DAD

## Linda G. Alvarez

Candescence Media
HALF MOON BAY, CALIFORNIA

www.CandescenceMedia.com

Book Layout ©2013 BookDesignTemplates.com

Ordering Information:
Quantity sales. Special discounts are available on quantity purchases by corporations, associations, and others. For details, use the above email address with subject line: "Special Sales Department."

Camino notes: walking the way with Dad/ Linda G. Alvarez. —1st ed.
ISBN 978-0-9900219-0-2

# Contents

*For Dad*

*Thanks for following in my footsteps . . .*
*the way a shepherd walks behind his flock.*

# Acknowledgements

I could not have walked the Camino or created this memoir without the help and generosity of friends and family.

I am grateful for the joy that Erin Essenmacher brings to my life, for her donated air miles, and her heroic patience during the reservation-making process.

Knowing that my clients were in the wise and capable hands of Diane Turriff for the two months I was away meant that I could walk without worry tethering me to the world of work. No words can express how precious that gift was to me.

My sweetheart, Ric Alvarez, was – as always – encouraging and supportive, helping me with plans and with "re-entry" into daily life upon my return.

My sister, Gayle Evers, amazes me. Her help bringing the book to fruition has smoothed an otherwise steep and rocky learning curve. What would I do without her sharp eyes, computer skills, and loving support? I'm glad I haven't had to find out.

And, of course, there's Dad. For years I'd toyed with the idea of walking the Camino de Santiago. It remained merely an idea until Dad made the firm decision to go himself. Thanks, Dad, for getting me up from the desk, away from the screens, and out into real life and adventure.

Linda G. Alvarez

# CHAPTER 1

# Beginnings

This is the story of my Camino. I walked with my 82-year-old father, Harold, so it is partly a story about his Camino too—but (obviously) from my limited perspective. If you want to know what his Camino was like, you'll have to ask him.

I've pieced together the story using blog posts that I wrote while we were walking, journal entries from my own and my father's journals, and my own best recollections. At times, I've quoted these sources (with some minimal editing). Each source—when quoted—appears in its own, distinctive font as follows: *Linda's Journals,* `Harold's Journals,` The Blog.

The test of any relationship is whether the pair can travel together. Dad and I can travel together. One of the things that helps is that neither of us expects the other to be a perfect companion—just a steady and happy one. I hope he will forgive me for the things that went through my mind and that I share here. I expect that he felt similar irritants and had thoughts about my absurdities along the way and I am grateful that he let them slide rather than making them into points of friction between us. I've included my own inner monologue not as a complaint, and not to say anything about him—but to give the full picture of my experience. My unworthy thoughts reflect my own shortcomings, not his. He was (and still is) a hero on the journey.

If you meet an American on the Camino de Santiago, you'll probably find that they've seen 'the movie.' The movie is *The Way* by Emilio Estevez starring his Dad, Martin Sheen. The pilgrimage to Santiago has been steadily growing in popularity over the last decade—partly due to several books (Paulo Coehlo's *The Pilgrimage*, *My Camino* by Canadian Sue Kenney, *I'm Off Then: Losing and Finding Myself on the Camino de Santiago* by German comedian Hape Kerkeling) and now The Movie. I think these books and the film reflect a hunger in the modern human across cultures, Western and Eastern. The Camino is enjoying a growing popularity among South Koreans (we were told the pilgrimage is good to have on one's resumé).

Pilgrimage is a concept slowly being retrieved by our modern culture from particular religions (in the case of the Camino, Catholicism). It is being applied by seekers—not only those who have 'a Faith' but also seekers who just have faith in some dimly glimpsed otherness, and by seekers with fading faith that this mysterious otherness is good and powerful enough to overcome the all too evident worldly crap-fest.

I can count on one finger the number of pilgrims we met who could answer the question, "Why are you on Camino?" with anything more than, "I don't know. I just felt like I had to do it." It seems to begin as a vague sense of aspiration—"I wish I could do that," "I wonder if I could do that," "I would do it, *except* [fill in the blank with some life-anchoring imperative]," until suddenly, a gap appears in the tightly woven fabric of daily life. A layoff, a graduation, or just a sudden vision of how it could be arranged...and the pilgrim finds herself at the sporting goods store trying on boots, online arranging international travel, and on the phone explaining as best she can to those who will stay behind and make sure the potted plants don't die. Those who watch her prepare begin to feel the tug of the possible, and she hears many a wistful, "That sounds so great. Good for you!"

I had been aware of the Camino de Santiago for a very long time. The first time I considered walking it was in my twenties. I bought some books about it and left them on the shelf having only read the introductions. But I carried the books with me for thirty years. Everywhere my life took me, I took the books about the Camino. "One day we'll do that," my husband and I promised one another, but neither of us could imagine doing it, and as we aged it became less and less likely that we would have the strength or drive to actually go for it.

Then one day, on our weekly Sunday Skype call, my father asked me if I had ever seen *The Way*. What had been dying embers revived to glow and burgeon into an energy source. I began to plan. And then I began to open the gap I'd need in my tightly constructed routine. And then, I was off.

## Blog Entry[1] — August 29, 2012

How We Come To Be Walking the Camino:
Harold Tells the Story

On February 21, 2012, I went to my home mailbox and was surprised to find a Netflix DVD entitled *The Way* starring Martin Sheen. I had not heard of the movie nor did I order it. I read the blurb on the envelope and it appeared to be about hiking.

Since Linda and I take a hiking vacation every two or three years, I assumed she had the movie sent to me so I called to thank her.

Linda said she had not heard of the movie and did not send it. So far, I have been unable to get anyone to confess to having sent it.

I watched the movie and discovered it was about a man walking the Camino de Santiago carrying the ashes of his son who had started his own pilgrimage but died on the first day.

I had never heard of the Camino de Santiago. I quickly researched it online. I then called Linda to tell her to watch this excellent movie and told her what I had discovered about the Camino de Santiago. I told her that St. James was the patron saint of Spain, that his symbol was the scallop shell, and that all the pilgrims who make the 500 mile pilgrimage carry a scallop shell visible somewhere on their person to indicate that they are pilgrims.

Linda said, "Dad, you do know that in our family coat of arms there are three scallop shells don't you?"

"No, tell me about them."

"During medieval times, three Graham knights made this pilgrimage and that is why the scallop shells were included in our coat of arms."

"Maybe I should make this pilgrimage," I said.

"Dad, it's more than that." (Linda's husband, Ric, is of Spanish descent.) "Do you know where Ric's family is from?"

"Not a clue."

"From Galicia—where the cathedral that is at the end of the pilgrimage and that holds the relics of St. James is located."

"Maybe we both need to make this pilgrimage." I answered.

"I think so."

"When do we leave?"

We each began to try to get into condition to make the pilgrimage.

---

## What *is* a pilgrimage?

I had a sense that I should know what 'pilgrimage' was all about before I actually made one. The concept seemed vaguely mystical—like I should expect epiphanies and miracles, undeserved forgiveness and liberation as a result of the effort. I felt like I'd be trying to cheat my way into heaven if I believed that pilgrimage would buy me a *Get Out of Jail Free* card from The Supreme Being. This was my impression of what medieval folks believed about pilgrimage—absolution in return for sufficient suffering—a sort of do-it-yourself punishment program, penitence physicalized and performed publicly, which I found uncomfortably showy when reflecting on the Sermon on the Mount.

I just didn't believe I could 'work off' my sins and blunders. I've messed up a few times and people have gotten hurt. How could I imagine that walking a pretty much random five hundred miles in Spain was going to have any curative impact on that reality?

So if I couldn't convince myself that walking the Camino would bring absolution, what the hell was I doing? What was this impulse to pilgrimage? What was it in the idea of pilgrimage that impelled me to participate? Honestly, I had no idea. It just seemed like the thing to do.

I turned fifty in 2008, so I suppose the whole midlife thing was a big part of my going. I found that upon reaching fifty, life's final horizon ceased receding the way it always had before. Now I can measure my approach to it. I can see that I am getting closer to it every day, and that makes me look with new eyes at what I do that fills the remaining time. Feeling like a cliché, I search for meaning and I check to see if each imperative in my life actually aligns with what really matters to me.

I imagined that I'd get to think about all this on the Camino. Hours and hours of walking would mean hours and hours of thinking and considering those questions we dash past on most days: "What really matters? What do I really want to be doing with my remaining time? When I look back on my life, what will I want to see? What would I be sad to see?"

I would be leaving behind a lot of responsibilities. Well, deferring them for a couple of months, not really quitting or losing them. Maybe that was what pilgrimage was about— walking into oneself, walking with one's own mind and body without the other bits of life that obscure awareness of the simple, basic personal truths.

Planning began. Practice walking started strong and dedicated, and petered out as the departure date grew near. I found I didn't have time to walk because I was trying to clear the decks so I could be gone for two months. I told myself that I was in good enough shape. I could carry my 20-lb. pack six miles and seemed to be walking at about 2.5 miles per hour when I did go out on the path. Of course, I was walking on flat terrain, either paved or beaten smooth, and the weather is always a cool 68–73 degrees Fahrenheit here in Northern California. But that's not such a big deal, right?

I tried to imagine what would be needed. Reading memoirs of others who have walked the Camino, I began checking the dates of their walks. Did they go in the last two years? Did they travel during the months I would be there? I was reading for weather, for terrain, for details about sleeping, eating, and laundry.

Dad was doing the same and making notes in his Brierley guidebook.[2] We continued to talk via Skype every Sunday morning, trading tips we'd found in books and blogs, and comparing equipment purchases. Dad was a project planner for Exxon for much of his career, so I abdicated to him all responsibility for deciding on the daily itinerary. Whatever he thought about how far to walk each day, where to stay, and what route to choose (when there were choices), I'd just go with that.

I was setting out on this effort without really taking into account that word—effort. Perhaps my 'don't look too closely' blindness was necessary. If I really let myself think about the size of the whole effort, my courage might fail. So, blithe ignore-ance was my solution. Anything that Dad was willing to take on that helped me avoid awareness of the harsh realities I was signing up for—good on him. Rose-colored glasses? Check. They were in the pack. I'd been practicing wearing them for years.

The plan was that Dad and I would spend a year preparing and then do our Camino in April and May of 2013. I figured it would take me that long to save up enough to cover the trip expenses plus the two months of income that I'd be foregoing while away.

Preparation that includes buying new clothes and equipment is always fun for me, so I plunged into the shopping experience with gusto. My first Camino purchases were boots and rain gear. My husband, Ric, and I had gone to REI to buy my boots. I knew I needed to be testing the boots well before hitting the Camino. Every memoir I read included a heavy focus on feet—foot care, foot trauma, and the fine and foul qualities of the walkers' boots and sandals.

What I found when we arrived at the store was that the all-weather gear was on clearance, so—after choosing a pair of boots and putting them on to wear around the store testing them for fit—I started digging through all the Gortex. I came across a pair of rain pants with zippers that ran all the way up the side seams of each leg (highly recommended in one of the memoirs), and they were in my impossible-to-find size (13 Petite). The price was slashed in half. It seemed like a sign. Ric and I dug through the raincoats and I chose one with a hood and with both zipper and snaps to close the front against wind. I left the store with boots, socks, raincoat and rain pants, ready to test them in what remained of Northern California's rainy season.

My training program consisted of walking the Pacific Coast trail that runs along the cliff tops overlooking the ocean. To get to it, all I have to do is walk out our front door, go around the corner, across a field and there I am. Super. In the rainy season (November through April), the path across the field becomes a long mud puddle, about 3–4 inches deep. The wind whips across the Pacific bringing rainstorms that shake our house. I rejoiced in the lousy weather and muddy field. Perfect testing ground for my shiny new boots and rain gear.

I started with walking four miles a day along the trail wearing my rain gear and coming home very proud of myself. I was not yet carrying a pack. I figured I would start easy and build up my strength. I didn't want to go too strong too soon and end up with injury. I also was waiting to buy the pack until I'd collected all the gear I planned to take. Knowing what all needed to fit into the pack would help me know what capacity pack to purchase.

As I read more books and did more online research looking for advice about what to take along on the Camino, I began to reconsider the hooded raincoat. The guidebooks and memoirs recommended a hooded rain poncho that would cover me and my pack, would be easy to put on in a sudden downpour and (I read with interest) could double as a portable screen for a woman who found herself needing to pee on a bald prairie. Given the fact that every ounce needed to be considered for its merit, I decided to pack the rain pants and poncho and leave the raincoat behind. It was my first choice between looking cute and being practical.

Early on in my preparations, I pretty much ditched all hope of looking good while on Camino. I made choices about clothes solely on the basis of practicality—wash-n-dry-ability, weight, pocket placement, etc. I scorned taking cosmetics, telling myself that they would be the epitome of unnecessary weight in the pack. Looking back, I think I could have given myself a little more comfort and primp than I did. By the end of five hundred miles and two months walking alongside other women who managed to look pretty damned cute wearing their cosmetics and colorful, fitted shirts, I was heartily tired of looking like a scruffy drudge in mud colored, shapeless clothes.

If I was to do it again—and I don't imagine that I will—I'd allow more concessions to my love of color, and attractive personal appearance. Think about it. If you are going to wear the same clothes day in and day out for a month and a half, no matter what they look like, you are going to hate them by the end of the walk, but you can *start out* liking them. The only place I would urge the ego to let go of appearances is in the choice of boots.

I'm a little vain about my small feet, and when I saw how neat and petite they looked in a snug pair of boots, I was sold. Then I started walking the miles in those cute little darlings. In short order, I found I had blisters rising on heels and ankles and toes. This would never do. Back I went to the store where I relinquished my vanity and bought a pair of boots that were a size larger than what I normally wore. On the first day walking in the new boots, I was amazed. The soles cushioned and supported my feet while the rest of the boot provided a shelter without pressing on my toes or arches.

I cannot emphasize this enough. *If you are going to walk far distances, buy boots that are shelters rather than wrappers for your feet.* If your toes touch the front or tops of the boots, those are not the boots for you. I met several women on the Way who were in agony from having their toes pounding against the inside front of their boots with every downhill step. Toenails were being lost. It was not pretty. I am grateful that I left my 'dainty feet' vanity behind. I walked the whole Way without blisters, rejoicing daily over the sturdy support and shelter of my boots.

## Linda's Journal

*March 11, 2012 –*
*Have spent the day reading about how to pack for the Camino. Walked to and from breakfast (two miles total) and notice a back-ache...but I have to start where I am!*

*Downloaded Shirley MacLaine's book about traveling the Camino—a bit scattered, but interesting thoughts sprinkled in, as well as helpful description of the trail and* refugio *(shelter) realities. She mentions getting 'oriented' to the Divine...it makes me think about navigational orientation—magnetic north. It also triggered a thought about how the profound shift in daily life (few possessions, no client demands, walking rather than driving) would recalibrate the mind and body and spirit to a different rhythm—different from our modern, digital, frenetic pace. I can feel my own yearning for it.*

> *"No other pilgrim I spoke to could explain why he or she was walking. It was a subject that came up every night in the refugios. There had been an impulse, almost a compulsion, that had guided us to drop our lives, put everything in suspension and come to Spain, and none of us knew why."[3]*

*This is how I am experiencing the plan to walk the Camino. I've half expected to do it for many years. Ric has talked about riding it on horseback, and then, the movie was sent to Dad—and off we go. It is clearly more than a pipe dream. The pieces continue to fall into place. Equipment I'll need is on sale and in my size, a friend has agreed to take over my client-service duties when I'm away; and, perhaps more telling, I've begun walking—a lot. It is astonishing. I feel like I'm being carried by the river's flow—doing one thing at a time as the current brings me to it.*

*March 18 –*
*Took a long walk, nearly 4 miles this afternoon. My feet were sore by the time I arrived home...my gear (jacket, hat, boots) kept me warm and dry all the way even though a very strong wind was blowing.*

*March 20 –*

*Shirley MacLaine's book got a bit loony for me. Thankfully, my friend J. Kim Wright put me onto a book by a Canadian lawyer, Julie Kirkpatrick, called* Camino Letters *about her walk. I'm enjoying that.*[4]

*March 21 –*
*I've been reading* Camino Letters *and, in one letter, she mentions grace. For me, grace is both a concept and a practice. "Concept" because of the Christian doctrine: Jesus died for our sins and God extends grace—a sort of Pardon Program for sinners. God still loves you and deems (or re-deems) you to be valuable and valued, worthy rather than damned. "Practice" because, while I find it challenging (mostly impossible) to (a) imagine God as a person-like being who issues pardons and (b) to imagine my own failures as in any way pardonable, I find it natural and often easy to have compassion and forgiveness towards others—to not hold their failings against them, to deem and re-deem them worthy and beautiful and valuable and valued. When I don't find it natural, I practice grace. The one person to whom I find it consistently impossible to extend or practice grace for is myself.*

*All this has triggered the memory of a time when I insisted to Ric that he should not reject or feel badly about receiving a wonderful gift just because he felt he didn't deserve it. "Maybe," I thought as I read today, "maybe I should notice that I have made myself unable to enjoy my blessed and wonderful life because I'm so busy feeling unforgivable, trying to adequately punish myself for what I imagine other people believe I've done wrong or failed to live up to."*

*I walked in the rain this morning, really more a heavy mist than true rainfall, but wet and cold and very windy...and my gear kept me warm and dry.*

*March 23 –*
*I've read some more of* Camino Letters *and find a lot in it that resonates,*

> *"It is not that I am unhappy about practicing law—there are many things that I love about it. I just spend too much of my time doing it, that's all. And it limits me from being able, or being allowed, to think about the world in any other way."[5]*

*She struggles with allowing herself to experience and believe in mystical occurrences. I know how she feels. I both yearn for and shy away from mystical experiences. I love them and then worry about my sanity.*

*March 28 –*
*I really feel as though a major shift is happening. "Work," for me, is changing. It appears to be increasing—more clients, more tasks—and, at the same time, my attention moves away from it. I think something is about to shift in a very big way and I don't know how to prepare myself for the unknowable, other than to let go of believing I need to know what's next—while planning to walk away from everything come April 1, 2013.*

*March 29 –*
*"Why are you walking the Camino? What motivates me in the first place to be out here and what is pushing me forward day after day and indeed what is at the heart of my walking prayer as I trek along?" (from* To the Field of Stars [6]*)*

*March 31 –*
The Pilgrimage as a metaphor is far from subtle. I'm noticing a longing for a different focus and rhythm—transcending the Almighty Dollar—connecting to life as it is lived (not just observing from the mind).

*April 15 –*
I've been reading Jack Hitt's book about the Camino, and he begins with an examination of "pilgrimage."[7] Pilgrim is a word that has been coming up a lot. It is the title of David Whyte's new book of poetry.[8] Pilgrimage—a very long walk, a minimalist experience for the 'strategic mind,' an exit from the normal, strategy-focused, neon-distracted modern culture world. I would love to take the trip and I plan to. The saving and arranging has begun. Who is the undistracted Linda? Dare I discover her?

The Camino de Santiago follows the path of the Milky Way (they say) to the edge of the earth.

Bought a new pair of boots after a six mile walk with Ric today. He and I went over to REI where, as it happened, today was the final day of "20% off one item." On top of the 20% discount, I had a $28 dividend to spend—so I bought a $170 pair for $119. Nice.

*April 16 –*
6 miles walked in my new boots. Not bad at all.

*April 30 –*
Trying to get to April of next year so that for two months I can walk away and be NOTHING but a Pilgrim.

*May 1 –*

*Thinking about the pilgrimage, about walking out of the roles and responsibilities that tend to harden around one as an identity—the function of time (2 mos.) and effort (500 miles), the shift of context so complete...well, almost complete. It will be me and Dad together. Hopefully, it will all serve to untangle, even unravel falsehood from Truth, facade from being. And what will be the plan for the after-pilgrim? Pre-pilgrim is struggling to set up habits of meditation and community, connection and solace, solitude and rest. Pilgrim will just have to cope—immersion mindfulness training. Post-pilgrim, the return to context, will be very interesting.*

*May 11 –*

*I went last night to the Stanford Campus to hear David Whyte. His new book of poetry (I found out) is in large part about the Camino de Santiago. Amazing. I had not made that connection when I saw the title of the collection. It turns out this new collection has poems about John O'Donohue and poems about the Camino. It was a lovely evening. My new friend, Anna, met me there and we enjoyed the evening together. Afterwards, I met her partner, Margaret.*

*May 26 –*

*Reading another Camino memoir,* I'm Off Then. *Looking outward and inward is sometimes done simultaneously. Walking in land-scape, natural settings, with head and eyes up, while Open-Empty-Receptive towards the window within. The outer Divine calls forward the inner Divine. "The eye with which you see God, is God's eye seeing you"—M Eckhart.*

*That looking up and out + opening inner channels (by emptying and silence) = connection with That Which Can Be Recognized But Nev-*

*er Named—it is 'satyagraha' (holding fast to Truth).[9] This, I think, is what the pilgrimage is about, sustained outward + inner silence/emptying. It is also the life of the artist (the poet, the painter, sculptor, dancer, musician). It is a connection and flow our technology-dominated lives seem designed to obscure—a connection buried by noise and words and information, a deluge of staticky, collaged, man-made sound and story, created to divert the mind, persuade, indoctrinate.*

*It feels like it will take many, many hours and miles for all 54 years of the chaos to run out and down to silence from within. It will be 55 years by the time we walk next year. So many stories and certainties and distractions to dissipate, pare down life and living to the current instant, the pack on the back not nearly the weight and drag that the mental conditioning and habits are. Memory—so constantly misused as punisher, degrading self-description—will that empty and silence itself? There may be a conscious-stilling component, the practice of noticing and pausing and redirecting attention. This becomes part of the practice of walking that I do to get my physical body in shape, strong enough and resilient enough to make the trek.*

*June 2 –*
*What I'm noticing is an inability to BE without turning on or turning to Computer-Email-Social media. Never has 'be here now' been so challenging. We can so easily be in a 'virtual' world. We don't even need our imaginations any more to escape our reality. Phantom lives are created for us, fed to us. We begin to believe we are having impact and making connections; yet we are sitting alone, not even thinking our own thoughts, just experiencing and following what is projected onto us and into us by the Virtual Info Feed.*

*June 10 –*
*Took a 3 mile walk yesterday and was happy to find that it was*
*unchallenging. I'd been worried that my long break from daily trek-*
*king would have put me back at Noodle One status. Today I'll try a*
*longer walk. While walking I tried to hold my attention on physical*
*sensations—visual, tactile, smell, sound. I noticed a lot of wandering*
*mind, but kept trying to bring attention and focus back. Also tried to*
*be aware of posture.*

## Change of plans

Dad and I were having our Sunday Skype conversation, exchanging ideas about what we were taking and which books
we'd read and liked (or not). He began saying, "I'm ready to go.
I wish we could go right now." After we hung up, I started
thinking about what he'd said.

Walking to brunch at a local beachside restaurant (three
miles there and three miles back) with Ric and our lovely
friend Erin, it hit me that my dad was eighty-two years old
and he was expressing a sense of urgency about getting started
on the Camino. The only reason we were waiting was that I
wanted to save up the money beforehand to cover the trip, but
there really was no other reason to wait. Then it occurred to
me, Ric and I were debt-free. I could borrow the money from
the bank and pay it back after I returned from Camino. I told
Ric and Erin what I'd decided. I felt exhilarated. Over mimosas
and french toast, Erin made a gift to me of her unused air
miles to help defray the travel costs. Wow. I gratefully and
enthusiastically accepted. Such an amazing gift. So much love.

When we got back from brunch, I sat down at the computer and emailed Dad.

> I was thinking about what you said this morning, "can't wait to get started on the Camino," and it started me wondering...If I can get the $$ together, would you be up for going this Sept/Oct? Would that be possible for you? I was going to start looking into whether it might be possible for me, but thought I should check to see if it is something you'd be up for if I did manage to wangle the finances? Just a wild idea...Linda

> You bet. I would prefer September because it's further from winter if that suits you. I would love to go this year...Harold

That Monday, I went to the bank and within two hours the loan was approved. Decision made. Momentum increased.

Then there was a dreadful turn of events.

---

## Linda's Journal

*July 13 –*

*Dustin Alvarez died this week. I think it was on Monday. I'm not sure because it happened in Alaska and Candy and Joe (and Jesse) were in Montana. Mary called on Tuesday night to tell us. Over the course of the day on Wednesday, we learned that it was an accidental gunshot—by his own hand—joking around with a gun he thought was not loaded. Horror. Disbelief. And waves of grief that surprise us with stealthy oppression. He was only 26 years old.*

*Also, between last Thursday and yesterday, Dad and I committed to walking the Camino this Sept/Oct. Plane tickets are booked. Will need to figure out trains and hotels. Need to pull out what I plan to*

*pack, then go and buy a pack, and keep walking, and keep working*
*to make as much do-re-mi as I can to help finance the trip. I've bor-*
*rowed to cover the 2 months lost income, the debt to be paid back over*
*2 years (or sooner if possible).*

---

Ric left for Montana to be with his brother Joe and I followed a few days later. This unbelievable loss shattered everyone who knew Dusty. Shell-shocked, we all did what we could
to keep one another breathing and eating. To bring Dusty
home from Alaska, they had to cremate his body. When the
ashes arrived, Joe and Candy asked me if I would carry some
with me on the Camino and leave them at Finisterre in Galicia, the Alvarez family home place.

Of course I would. I took the precious little container and
packed it carefully away, knowing that carrying it meant I
would not give up along the way. Now I was certain I would
walk the Camino all the way to the end. No quitting.

# Notes

[1] It quickly became evident that there would be many folks at home wanting to keep up with how Dad and I were doing on our adventure. I worried that Mother would be inundated by email and phone queries, and would get no peace, so I set up a 'blog spot' page where I could post news from the Camino as we walked, using my iPhone whenever we encountered wifi access. I started posting on July 28 in order to test the process, work out any bugs and give all our friends time to find the blog and learn how to read it and comment. www.caminonotes.blogspot.com

[2] Brierley, John. *A Pilgrim's Guide to the Camino De Santiago: St. Jean, Roncesvalles, Santiago : The Way of St. James : The Ancient Pilgrim Path Also Known as Camino Francés.* Forres, Scotland: Camino Guides/Findhorn, 2012. Print. (Camino Guides, www.caminoguides.com)

[3] MacLaine, Shirley. *The Camino: The Journey of the Spirit.* New York: Pocket, 2000. 73.

[4] Kirkpatrick, Julie. *The Camino Letters: 26 Tasks on the Way to Finisterre.* Millbrook, Ont.: Pyxis, 2010. Print.

[5] Ibid., 141.

[6] Codd, Kevin A. *To the Field of Stars: A Pilgrim's Journey to Santiago De Compostela.* Grand Rapids, MI: William B. Eerdmans Pub., 2008. Print.

[7] Hitt, Jack. *Off the Road: A Modern-day Walk down the Pilgrim's Route into Spain.* New York: Simon & Schuster Paperbacks, 2005

[8] Whyte, David. *Pilgrim: Poems.* Langley, WA: Many Rivers, 2012. Print.

[9] "Satyagraha" is the word that M. Gandhi coined to describe his practice of nonviolence. Many authorities state that the word literally translates as "hold fast to Truth."

# CHAPTER 2

# Final Planning Stages

D ad and I began booking airline tickets. The plan was for me to fly from San Francisco to Houston (where he and Mom live), spend the night and then he and I would fly together to Spain. I reserved a seat on a flight to London and on a flight from there to Madrid, and I sent the info to Dad. My sister booked his travel to match mine.

## Linda's Journal

*July 17 –*

*Am trying to get my head around the fact that I'm leaving on Sept 5 to be gone until Nov 5! Dad and I will be on the Camino together.*

*That last sentence stalled my brain by flooding it with 'need to' lists. Work on remembering my Spanish, walk, pack & prepare, contact Diane T about serving clients during my absence, alert clients that I'll be away for 2 mos., clear the decks of all backlogged work. Slow down to go fast. If I panic, I'll flounder…*

*July 18 –*
*I bought the pack and walking stick yesterday. Wow. Hostel in Madrid booked. Pack and all the bits mostly purchased...need the sleeping bag. Wow.*

*July 26 –*
*I woke up scared about the Camino, about the walking, the expense, the time, and wondering why I'm doing it, and what meaning I will find in the doing and the aftermath.*

*July 28 –*
*38 days. Yesterday, I took the fully loaded pack out for a 4 mile hike. That was just at the limit of 'comfort' for me. I'll try and go again today.*

---

## Blog Entry — Wednesday, July 28, 2012

Preparations—Weighing Everything

Airline reservations are made, hostel reserved in Madrid for Sept 7, boots, pack, sleeping bag...my life has become a checklist. It is actually SEVERAL checklists—a list of checklists.

- o   Client Work to be done before I leave

- o   Business Sustenance Arrangements - keeping things ticking along

- o   Home and Personal Affairs to get in order - just in case...

- o   Travel and Lodging plans - there and back again

- o   Kit for the Walk

I'm weighing everything that goes into the pack. I'm trying to keep the weight on my back (knees really) to under 15 lb. I find myself weighing my towel, my toothbrush, my shoestrings...As the book says, "To Walk Far, Carry Less."[1]

The metaphor is annoyingly unsubtle as I consider how much communications equipment to take along. At a minimum, I'll take the iPhone[2] and a charger cord (and adapter plug). I plan to disable phone/data and use only wifi. It is a difference without a distinction though—thanks to Skype. With Skype, I will be able to make and receive phone calls.

The next question is whether to take a solar charger for the phone (add .5 lb. in weight). The truth is, this question is more about how readily connectable I want to be while I'm on the pilgrimage road. Can I risk losing connection for more than a day or two? Do I really need to be in constant connection? Do I want to be?

I'm resisting what I really know deep down—that a crucial aspect of pilgrimage is the separation from one's daily norm and comfortable identities. How separated am I prepared to be? Dare I separate from my beloved identities and risk trekking out into a world of radio silence for two months?

My busy mind is convinced that if I'm not pedaling, the world won't keep turning properly. Maybe that's the experiment inherent in a two-month pilgrimage. I have to admit, I'm pretty scared about stepping out the door and leaving the business I've built and career I've nurtured to the care of others for 56 days.

Would carrying connectivity guarantees along with me be carrying a safety net or dragging a tether? Thoughts?

---

My sister begged me to take the solar charger. She was worried we'd get stranded out in a wilderness and not be able to call for help. I carried it on a few test runs and decided that it didn't work well enough to justify a full half-pound of weight. I was already sawing the handle off my hair brush and packing only half a bar of soap in the effort to reduce the weight in my pack. I decided to walk without the solar charger.

As the departure date moved closer, and in the wake of Dusty's death, I found my walks took on a contemplative tone. I was turned more inward, pondering questions about that horizon we all believe is so far away, and at which some arrive unexpectedly early.

## Linda's Journal

*July 29 –*

*While walking yesterday, I felt myself reach an acceptance that there have been very dark passages in my life's journey. Times when I wandered into hells and allowed myself to stay, allowed others to wander in with me; but these dark passages need not disqualify me from happiness, contribution, participation. In fact, they qualify me to be kinder, more careful, compassionate, and aware...*

*Just sitting and remembering that "reality" is obscured by shadows masquerading as Truth, ground, God, Love, Right...shadows falter and pass...beware of 'certainty' about anything...the questions hold the lantern.[3]*

*July 31 –*

*I've only gone 4 miles per day since taking on the fully loaded pack, and I've slowed down as well. The 4 miles took 2 hours yesterday. My mind skitters off into questions about how to make the pack work better...I'm wondering about carrying a sketchbook and pencils. I know that I tend to have an urge to sketch when I travel. There is plenty of space in the pack for it. Will I love it for its worth in weight? I think that aside from weight, the packing and re-packing of bits must wear thin along the road. What will I be pulling out daily? Sleep gear, personal hygiene and laundry, daily walking clothes. What will I be carrying that isn't daily? Rain & cold weather gear. What will I need easy access to on the trail? Weather gear, water bottle, toilet paper, journal?, phone, whistle.*

*August 3 –*
*I've not walked the last two days, and I've gone a bit radical with the hair color (added blue, teal, purple strands)—breaking out of molds and pushing envelopes of expectations.*

*August 5 –*
*I packed all the clothes I imagine I'll need, all else and sundry; and the pack with water weighs 17 lb. I walked 6 miles carrying the pack and am pretty tired out, but feel myself returning to energy and think I might be able to do a bit more walking if it was required of me. Went downtown in Half Moon Bay and bought scallop shells to carry for Joe, Candy and Jesse.*

---

Every pilgrim on the Camino carries a scallop shell, the symbol of St. James for whom 'Santiago de Compostela' is named. I decided to carry additional scallop shells for Dusty's family, one each for his mother, father and brother. I found three different shells at the local shell shop and using jewelry-making wires, I created holders with loops that allowed me to tie them to my pack.

## Linda's Journal

*August 11 –*
*The day of client work yesterday was full in the sense that it set up more work to be done—and done sooner—adding to the wonderfully building pressure of 'get this done before I leave.' I have been getting things done, just not all that I'd like or not enough to seem like any meaningful deck space has been cleared.*

*I wasn't able to walk the 6 miles yesterday. My body actually felt fatigued as though I had done...odd. I'll walk it today. Maybe I'm turning the corner where the long walk will invigorate rather than fatigue me. (Hope so)*

*August 14 –*
*Three weeks till the trip begins. I chose not to walk yesterday. Will have to walk today...also need to do my Spanish lessons...*

*August 19 –*
*Seventeen days until I leave for Spain. The packing and repacking continues. I change my mind about what to carry, I take everything out and weigh it again. I practice carrying it all. I practice opening and closing the pack on the trail. I've begun painting little watercolor sketches in the miniature notebooks I'm carrying. I went to the store to buy new insoles for my boots and came away with new boots. My feet hurt already and I wonder if I'm doing the right thing walking 6 miles a day with pack. They hurt in my sleep now. Well, I guess that's all part of the experience—enhances one's sense of the present moment.*

*I look at the calendar and see that this really is the last week of focus on non-Camino things. I'll need to 'buckle down' and get things cleared off the calendar.*

*August 20 –*
*I'm about to set out on a long meander across Spain. Pilgrimage has been forming for a year or so and now it comes to fruition.*

---

The boots I had been wearing to train for the walk were starting to feel broken down. The arch support was not holding up as much as I wanted. I went to REI looking for shoe inserts and discovered a pair of boots by the same maker that were a step up in sturdy from the ones I'd been wearing, so I bought a new pair of boots. Conventional wisdom warns against buying a new pair of boots right before a trek, but I knew the maker and was confident that the fit would be good. I chose to accept the risk that a fresh pair of boots might rub or pinch.

---

## Blog Entry — August 23, 2012

A Great Moment Knocks on the Door of Your Heart

In just under two weeks, I walk out the door and begin the journey on the Camino. Final preparations are underway. I'm unpacking and repacking. Where possible, I'm exchanging some items for others that weigh less. I'm walking to test the fit of clothes, boots and pack, and to test the fitness of my body.

What I can't really test is the fitness of my mind and spirit. I guess that is what the pilgrimage is for.

I try to imagine what the next two months will be like, what I will encounter on both the outer and inner paths. I admit to more than a little trepidation. I've been turning to favorite authors for what reassurance and encouragement I can find, such as this from John O'Donohue's *To Bless The Space Between Us* (*Benedictus* in the UK):

### A GREAT MOMENT KNOCKS ON THE DOOR OF YOUR HEART

*It remains the dream of every life to realize itself, to reach out and lift oneself up to greater heights. A life that continues to remain on the safe side of its own habits and repetitions, that never engages with risk of its own possibility, remains an un-lived life. There is within each heart a hidden voice that calls out for freedom and creativity. We often linger for years in spaces that are too small and shabby for the grandeur of our spirit. Yet experience always remains faithful to us. If lived truthfully and generously, it will always guide us towards the real pastures.[4]*

## Linda's Journal

*August 31 –*

*5 days until I leave for the Camino. The tasks on my to-do list are fewer, visits from friends increasingly on the schedule—trepidation and hope. I've been reading memoirs and blogs by former pilgrims, and their descriptions of the 'single-tasking' simplicity of the pilgrimage. I'm reminded of the Quaker song "'Tis a Gift To Be Simple." Here I go! It will be a heightened contrast, I think, because of the rush that has come in the last days before departure—rush and crowding of busy-ness.*

## Blog Entry — September 5, 2012

It requires more than a day's devotion...

In *Life Without Principle*, Thoreau wrote, "It requires more than a day's devotion to know and to possess the wealth of a day... Really to see the sun rise or go down every day, so to relate ourselves to a universal fact, would preserve us sane forever."

Today, I'm stepping out the front door and setting my feet on the pilgrim path. More than a day's devotion. I'm on my way to Houston to meet up with Dad, then—tomorrow—he and I will fly to Spain. We will make our way to the start of the Camino by way of Madrid > Pamplona and expect to be walking by Sunday. Together, we'll see the sun rise and go down every day for 500 miles.

From San Francisco to Houston, I'm carrying my pack and what I've come to think of as my "civilization bag" (the laptop, cosmetics, 'normal' clothes). I'll leave the civilization bag in Houston. Yes. I see the figurative as well as the practical meaning.

I'm scared. I turn once again to John O'Donohue:

*May my mind come alive today*
*To the invisible geography*
*That invites me to new frontiers*
*To break the dead shell of yesterdays*
*To risk being disturbed and changed.*

*May I have the courage today*
*To live the life that I would love,*
*To postpone my dreams no longer*
*But do at last what I came here for*
*And waste my heart on fear no more.*[5]

## Crossing the Continent & Atlantic

Flying with a backpack is a bit of a hassle. You can't just check it like a regular bag. The backpack has to either be shrink-wrapped in plastic or placed in a carrying case that doesn't have all those dangling straps and buckles to snag in the baggage handling machinery. This is a challenge for the trekker, because the bags designed for the job are expensive and heavy. I couldn't bring myself to spend $60 on a carrying case that weighed a whole pound and would just be dead weight in the pack all the way across Spain. Ric and I went searching for a laundry bag, something strong enough to hold up in baggage handling hell and cheap enough that I wouldn't mind tossing it into the trash once I arrived in Spain. We finally found just the thing at Bed, Bath & Beyond, a satchel designed for laundry that had a shoulder strap on the outside for easy carrying. It only cost $10. I bought one for Dad too. The problem was that my walking stick, even when it was fully collapsed, was just a little too long for the bag. I stretched and pulled and managed to close the thing around both pack and stick. I paid a price though. The outer bag was slightly torn when my pack arrived in Houston.

Dad's stick was also too long for the satchel. Fortunately, his ticket allowed him to check two bags without paying extra, so we went to the UPS store and bought a sturdy cardboard tube to pack our sticks in for the flights. I lashed the torn satchel tightly around my pack and prayed that it would hold up on the transatlantic trip.

## Harold's Journal

September 5, 2012

I finished training. From February 24, 2012 to September 5, 2012 I walked exactly 1000 miles.

Day 1. September 6, 2012

The plane out of Houston was delayed two hours.

Day 2. September 7, 2012

I arrived in London 8:46 AM. Linda and I knew we were not seated together from Houston to London but expected to be seated together from London to Madrid. However, when we arrived in London we discovered we were on different planes to Madrid. Linda went ahead and my plane was to follow in an hour and a half. But two of the passengers on my flight who checked bags didn't show. So the airline had to unload all the baggage and take their bags off. Then some of their fellow travelers decided to leave the plane too and it had to all be done again.

# Notes

[1] Ashmore, Jean-Christie. *Camino De Santiago: To Walk Far, Carry Less.* Lexington, KY: Walk Far Media, 2011. Print.

[2] The phone also doubled as a camera. To see more of the photos from our journey, go to http://www.candescencemedia.com/camino-notes.

[3] "The Question Holds The Lantern." *John O'Donohue.* Web. 06 Oct. 2013. http://www.johnodonohue.com/words/question.

[4] O'Donohue, John. *To Bless The Space Between Us: A Book of Blessings.* New York: Doubleday, 2008. 192. Print.

[5] O'Donohue, John. "A Morning Offering." *To Bless The Space Between Us: A Book of Blessings.* New York: Doubleday, 2008. 8-9. Print.

# CHAPTER 3

# Madrid > St. Jean

## Planes, Trains, & Buses

Having arrived in Madrid two hours before Dad, I collected my pack and sat on the floor of the baggage claim area resting and waiting. I've never been good at sleeping on planes, and this transatlantic flight was no exception. We'd been delayed in both Houston and Heathrow, and now, sitting on the cold tile floor of the Madrid airport, I was not willing to even doze while I waited for Dad. When he arrived, we gathered up his bag and the tube of sticks from baggage claim. I connected with the airport wifi and we called Mom using Skype to let her know we were safely arrived and united. Then we set out to find the metro train that would take us to the city center where our hostel was located.

Dad had mapped our metro route before leaving Houston, and pulled out a reference page with the Madrid metro map and his notes on stops and transfers. Once the very patient airport staff member had helped us operate the ticket dispensing machines in the metro station (located on a lower level of the airport), we boarded our first subway train and anxiously watched for the point of transfer. We disembarked at the first stop and started making our way to the platform where another line would carry us to the hostel. Metros have lots of stairs. Just sayin'.

When we were finally off the train and up on the earth's surface again, we found ourselves in the midst of surging rush hour crowds. Bumped and batted by hurrying Spaniards on congested sidewalks, we set out in the direction we thought would take us to the hostel. After a few blocks, we thought we might have taken a wrong turn. We retraced our steps and tried again. After about a half hour of wandering, we came to a pair of *policia* and Dad asked them for directions. They pointed us in the right direction and finally we arrived to find that our hostel was on an upper floor. No elevator.

With no sleep for more than 24 hours, I eyed the stairs and told myself I could haul the pack up because at the top of this stairway was my bed for the night. Up we went to be met with the news that they had given our room to someone else! Not to worry, the smiling host told us, they had a room for us at another location—only five minutes walk away. He pointed to a staff member who would lead the way for us.

Dad and I looked at one another. What I was thinking cannot be spoken aloud in polite company. Our host must have read my mind, because he immediately offered that our guide would carry Dad's pack for him. Dad refused the help. I did not. I handed over my pack to the young Romanian fellow and we set off on our walk, too weary to try and track directions.

We climbed more stairs up to an apartment that served as a bed and breakfast (without the breakfast). The proprietress assigned us to our rooms and handed over a set of keys—one each with our respective room numbers, and two others identified as 'front door of apartment' and 'front door of building.' We decided to rest a bit before heading out for dinner.

By the time we were ready to go for dinner, the proprietress of our B&B had left. We were alone in the place. We carefully locked the apartment and eased ourselves down the stairs to street level, but when we tried to open the door, we couldn't unlock it. The key turned in the lock, but the front door to the building would not open. Pushing, rattling, trying the key over and over, nothing would make the thing budge. Finally we discovered that there was a button far off to one side of the hallway, inset in the wall, which had to be pushed to release an electronic lock. Whew! Nearly done in by the efforts of the exit, we decided to eat someplace very close. Happily, there was a friendly café just across the street where we were able to navigate the menu with minimal struggle. The café's theme was American Television of the 1960's. Black and white photos of American TV personalities ranged the aqua walls. On a television in a high corner, an old episode of *The Munsters* provided background ambiance for our ham and egg sandwiches and salads.

Madrid was experiencing a record heat wave and the evening was still quite warm. Returning to our beds in the hostel I was grateful a small fan was provided, as the rooms were cramped and stuffy. Dad's was windowless. We said goodnight to one another and I lay down on my bed.

Sleep would not come. The hostel had wifi, so I pulled out the iPhone and posted my first Camino Note from the road. I also wrote a quick entry in my tiny 3" x 3" journal.

*September 7 – We left Houston at 6:30 PM Wed. (after*
*waiting in the airport from 3 PM) now it is 1 AM on Friday*
*morning in Madrid—25 hours later...a prosaic beginning of*
*mundane air and metro transportation.*

Dad tells me that more guests arrived at our Madrid hostel at about 2 AM and started a loud party. They kept him awake. I had finally fallen asleep by then and heard not a thing.

I dragged myself awake at 7 AM knowing that Dad and I had a train to catch somewhere in Madrid. St. Jean is a traditional starting point for the *Camino Frances* (the route that most pilgrims travel). It is in France and there were no trains that went all the way from Madrid to St. Jean, so we would have to stop somewhere short of the Spanish/French border and catch a bus. We were planning to take the train from Madrid to Pamplona and then catch a bus from there to St. Jean Pied de Port. We had not been able to book our tickets online or even confirm our information about options for transport, so we were doing this stretch based on schedules as we found them, buying tickets once we arrived at the appropriate depots.

We left our $10 satchels in our rooms at the hostel, gifts to the next inhabitants who might need them. We caught the metro to the train station where we managed to purchase tickets from machines in the lower lobby before settling in chairs in the station's only café. We took turns going to the counter to order breakfast. The café had free wifi, so I was able to check email and surf the web while we waited for our train departure time.

On the train, we watched as scenery flashed past: ancient stones, tiled roofs, a Roman aqueduct, flat walls in varying shades of bright, depending on sun or shadow. All were white or ochre. Each town was marked by its tallest structure, the bell tower. We watched as olive orchards, citrus orchards, vineyards and fields of scorched corn and burnt brown sunflowers, unharvested and rattling in the fields, slipped past our windows. We caught the occasional glimpse of pilgrims walking through the distant countryside and I tried to imagine Dad and myself on those same paths. How long would it take us to be back here traveling on foot?

From the station in Pamplona, we took a taxi to the bus station where we would wait and wait for the bus from Pamplona to St. Jean. Finally we boarded and held onto our seats as the huge bus wound up and around and over the Pyrenees on tiny, switchback roads. I was exhausted with travel and ready to be in St. Jean, the 'real' start of our trip.

## St. Jean Pied de Port

We arrived in St. Jean at about 7:30 PM and walked from the bus station into town searching for the Pilgrim Office where I could get a scallop shell to hang on my pack. Dad had his already. He had ordered it through the mail before we left the States. I had decided to wait and get a shell in St. Jean, but our late arrival thwarted my plans. I had just placed my hand on the door to the Pilgrim Office when a woman opened it from within and told me that they were locking the door. The office was closed and would not reopen until after 10 AM tomorrow—two hours after our planned departure time. She explained that they had been flooded with pilgrims all day and none of the staff had had a break. They were exhausted and would not allow me to even come in for a shell.

Exhausted. I knew the feeling, but all that mattered to her was her own fatigue. She closed the door firmly and locked us out. I was so disappointed. Now I would be setting out on the Camino without a shell. There was no time to look for one in the local shops. With the record crowds of pilgrims filling the town, getting our night's stay arranged was an urgent priority. Dad and I crossed the street and asked at a hostel whether they had room. No room. All full. Did the landlady have any suggestions for us? She pointed back down the hill we had just climbed and said, "Number 15."

So we walked down the cobbled Rue de Castille, passing sign after sign on hostel doors proclaiming, "*Complet*"—no rooms available. At last we came to Number 15, "Chez Habitones Hotel." The huge, ancient door was closed. We pushed it open and found ourselves in a long, dim hallway. There was nothing that looked like a reception desk or hotel office. It was just a long hall, like you'd expect to see in a private home. We took a few tentative steps forward, "Hello?" No response. We went further, past a massive wooden stairway, all the way to the back of the house. There were no signs of life. We turned around and were headed back to the front door when a side door popped open and a lady (in her 80's?) leant out to ask us in French if we were looking for a room. "Yes!" we said. She had one room left. She instructed us to take off our boots and leave them at the foot of the massive staircase.

We wanted to be sure there were two beds and in the course of that conversation (in a mix of French, Spanish, and English) she realized that we were father and daughter. Shifting from her former attitude of typically European nonchalance, Madame's face lit up with surprise and then amazement.

The next (inevitable) question was "How many years has your father?" And when I told her, "82," she threw up her hands and said, "*Ay! Que guapo!*" which means, roughly, "He looks great!" But her admiration did not stop there.

She continued to exclaim over Dad's beauty as she led us up three flights of ancient stairs to our (very nice) room. There she stayed with one hand on Dad's arm the whole time, chattering about how much she loves the U.S. and how gorgeous he was. There was kissing too (on the cheek). I was beginning to worry that things might be getting out of hand and was starting to look for a photo of Mom on my iPhone, but Madame eventually left with our payment for the room in hand.

Her name, it turned out, is Maria Camino. And the house she lives in and runs as a hostel for pilgrims was bought for her by her husband of seventy years with the money he earned in the seven years he worked as a shepherd in Nevada. She showed us a photo of him standing in the foreground with his border collie and the flock behind him.

After we'd settled ourselves into the room, we set out to find dinner. I could hear singing somewhere—a men's choir it sounded like—but we couldn't tell where it was coming from. St. Jean is a medieval town with tiny cobbled streets winding between tall, ancient buildings that seem to lean towards one another over the heads of pedestrians. We wandered along reading the chalkboard menus propped outside various cafés until we found one that seemed attractive. We were seated at a table in the back patio, under a cloth umbrella. I honestly don't remember what we ate. I was grateful to be sitting down and began to look around at the other diners. It appeared that almost all were pilgrims. Some were in boisterous groups, others were lone pilgrims savoring their meal in solitude. I wondered if we'd see any of them on the trail the next day.

Weary to the core, we returned to Number 15, took our showers and crawled into bed with lights out by 10 PM.

## Linda's Journal

*September 8 – 10:30 PM*
*We arrived in SJPdP too late for me to get a shell. Pilgrim Office was closed and we had to get a room, which took so long the other shops had closed. I'm really sad. I'm also very worried about tomorrow. I could hardly walk up the street slope today. How will I climb for 5 miles? And what if there is no room at Orisson? We'll have to walk all 17 miles. SCARED...DISAPPOINTED = feeling angry.*
*–sigh –*

The bathroom was on the floor below our room, so the middle of the night trip involved groping for the door, sliding my feet along the smooth wooden floor to the first step, then grasping the massive banister and creeping slowly down the unlit, creaking stairs, to another stealthy slide along the lower corridor to the bathroom where the automatic light dazzled sleepy eyes and rendered the return creep even more dark and treacherous. I had a wakeful night. I wrestled with worries about my capacity to make the journey.

I made a second trip to the loo at about 6 AM and returned to our room to find the lights on and Dad packing up and preparing to leave. I could have slept 'til noon, but the plan was to be on the trail as early as possible, so I followed his lead. As I was rearranging the contents of my pack, I came across my little parcel of watercolor supplies. There I found the scallop shell that I had brought with me from Half Moon Bay. It was destined to be my water bowl whenever I wanted to paint. Now it would serve double-duty as my pilgrimage shell too, if I could just figure a way to attach it to the outside of my pack. I don't know why it was so important to have a shell from the outset, but it was. We were packed and ready to go by 7 AM. Madame had told us that breakfast was at 8 AM and so we waited in the room, straining to hear if the house was yet awake. I made a one last pre-Camino note in my journal.

## Linda's Journal

*September 9 – 7:30 AM*
*About midnight, I decided that I don't want to do this. Then, an hour or so later, I (figuratively) squared my shoulders and decided to do it after all, come what may...The bells of the church rang at 7 AM and again at 7:30. I hear voices downstairs. We'll go soon.*

Happily, when we descended to the kitchen, Madame was there with the sliced baguette, jam and coffee that comprised 'breakfast.' At the table was an Italian couple—he a retired professor—on their second Camino trip. They had walked from León to Santiago some years ago and were now coming back to complete the earlier legs of the Route Frances.

The tiny meal left both Dad and me hungry and we had nothing in our packs for lunch, so as we walked through town we watched for a grocery or bakery. It was Sunday morning and the town was sleeping late. No shops were open.

# CHAPTER 4

# On The Road At Last:
# St. Jean > Orisson

---

## The Pyrenees

We walked out the door of Number 15 at about 8 AM and started up into the mountains. The morning was misty and still. As we walked across the bridge and up into the foothills, we saw other pilgrims ahead.

We passed a sign identifying our path as the "Route de Napoleon."

Leaning forward we began our ascent. At first we passed through neighborhoods. Then the houses were further apart with livestock in the adjacent pastures. We were walking on a paved road that began to  wind and grow steeper as the sun rose higher. Temperatures

44 •

kept pace with the rising sun and before long had risen to nearly 90 degrees Fahrenheit.

The hike started steep and grew steeper, until even the Germans were slowing down and commenting on the difficulty. At one point, we passed a young woman carrying her 11-month-old daughter in a sling, accompanied by the baby's teenaged uncle. They had paused along the side of the road to use the wide wooden slats of a barnyard fence as a diaper-changing table. Dad and I wondered at her fortitude to be carrying an infant up and over the Pyrenees. Later, the trio caught up with us and we all stopped to meet, greet, and take photos of what were likely the youngest and oldest pilgrims on the walk at present. We learned that they were from Ireland and were on vacation, planning to walk as far as they could in the days they had free before returning home.

I was slow. Very, very slow. The long trip from Houston, the lack of sleep and the inadequate breakfast were, for me, beginning to tell. Dad seemed unfazed. As the path grew ever steeper, he advised me that smaller steps took less energy than long ones. Like a bicyclist shifting into a low gear, I began shuffling along the steepest bits.

The scenery was spectacular. It was our trade-off for the heat. Many pilgrims cross the Pyrenees surrounded by a cold fog that cloaks the views. We had clear air and endless vistas. I stopped often to take photos with my iPhone that I kept in a pants pocket for easy access.

For a while we walked on dirt path, then emerged again onto pavement. Other pilgrims would overtake and pass us, muttering greetings and occasionally guessing at the distance remaining to reach Orisson.

As we walked, Dad would announce his estimates of how much further we had to go. I had to ask him to stop calculating out loud. I found it too discouraging to have him announce, "Three more miles!" just as I was hoping it was only about one more. I also had to ask him to stop supplying the counter to my attempts to cheer myself on. If I said, "Yeah! A downhill section!" he'd reply, "The thing about downhill is, you just have to go up again." Sigh.

"Not necessarily!" I'd answer, thinking to myself, "After all, we're going OVER the Pyrenees. There will be a big descent eventually." He complied with my request—chuckling.

Orisson is the only *albergue* (al-BEAR-gay) between St. Jean and Roncesvalles. I had read that reservations were recommended if one wanted to sleep there, but I hadn't been certain of the date we'd be starting our walk so I had not called ahead. From St. Jean to Orisson is five miles. Dad and I had expected it would be a nice, easy way to start the trip. As it turned out, with the heat and the steep grade, it took us a grueling 5 hours to get there.

We arrived around 1 PM and the place was a madhouse of pilgrims ordering lunch to eat out on the deck overlooking a spectacular view of the mountains. Dad found us a table and sat there while I went into the bar to see about food and sleeping arrangements.

I snagged an energetic young woman who seemed to be organizing the chaos and asked if they had two beds for the night. She told me they were full. I looked at her and said, "I'm walking with my father. He is 82 years old." She paused, then told me that all they had was a tent. They didn't have any mattresses for the tent. It was their last remaining 'emergency' shelter. I told her we'd take it. I went back out and told Dad. We spent the next hour or so getting lunch from the bar and drinking iced sodas.

After the lunch rush had subsided we connected with our bright and bouncing hostess. We pulled out our pilgrim passports and had the Orisson stamp added to the stamp Madame Camino had given us that morning (a hundred years earlier). The young hostess showed us the showers and gave us each a token to use to start the hot water. She warned us very carefully that once the token was inserted in the slot, the water would only be on for 5 minutes. After that it shut down automatically. One token = 5 minutes of shower, and only one token per pilgrim allowed.

She then led us up a steep, dusty slope to our tent. It was a two-person pup tent clinging to the hillside. Not quite level, it had two high-density foam mats crammed into its sweltering interior. Paradise. I was grateful to let go of my pack and not to be walking on. It was another twelve miles to Roncesvalles. Dad offered to keep going if I wanted to. I firmly declined and went to take my shower.

I was happy to discover that five minutes is plenty of time for a shower. That hot water felt like the height of luxury. Afterwards, I washed everything I had worn that day in the designated laundry sink and hung it all out on the line provided. Rows of socks and undies and T-shirts were already waving in the breeze. Dad and I joined our fellow pilgrims out on the deck where I pulled out my watercolors and tried in vain to capture the glorious scenery.

Dinner was served at three long tables lined on each side by benches. A sausage and bean stew with bread and rice was spooned into bowls and passed from hand to hand till every pilgrim had plenty. We introduced ourselves to our closest tablemates. Across from us sat Ellen and Carol. Ellen was from England and Carol from Victoria, Canada. To Dad's left was a woman from the U.S. who was delighted with him. I heard her say to him, "I could just kiss you all over!" I looked up and caught Carol's eyes, wide with amazement. I shrugged and said, "It happens all the time." Which is true. Something about my dad is magnetic. Ladies come up to him in stores, restaurants, airports, train stations, any- and everywhere, and tell him he's adorable. I don't see it myself. I think he's nice and smart and pretty good-looking, but I wouldn't think of him as the cuddly-adorable type. But more power to him if that's the effect he has on the ladies. Mom gets a kick out of it.

As the meal was ending, our hostess stood and explained that at Orisson the tradition was for each pilgrim to stand and say something about himself or herself. We were invited to say our name, where we were from, and then say something, or even sing if we felt moved to do so. Imagine my surprise when the first guys to speak from the far corner were Michael from Menlo Park, California, and Rick from San Mateo! Neighbors in California here on the Camino. Astonishing.

A delightful hour and a half ensued with story telling and laughter. The lady of the kisses and her traveling companion sang a song for the road. Dad got up and told about how he and I came to be on the Camino. Everyone wanted to know and then was amazed to learn his age. I don't remember what I said—I hope it was brief. At last the day was done and it was time for sleeping. Dad and I collected our clothes from the line (rain was predicted overnight) and scrambled up the hill to our tent.

Here's how Dad described the day's adventure:

---

## Harold's Journal

Day 4. September 9, 2012

We were up and ready to go at 7:30 in the morning in St. Jean, France. I slept well, feel good, weather is hot. Linda and I walked from St. Jean to Orisson. When we arrived in Orisson the albergue was full but they had one last tent left. We rented it. We had a wonderful lunch of marinated ham, salad, and french fries. We washed our clothes, took a hot shower, and went out to look at the beautiful scenery. Dinner was at 6:30 PM, breakfast will be at 7 AM. We ordered bocadillas for the walk tomorrow to be delivered at breakfast.

---

Stoic much?

We left the window flaps open because the night was still quite warm. I unfurled my sleeping bag and laid it on top of the foam mat, inflated my travel pillow and laid down to sleep. I bought that sleeping bag because it packed down to a really small size and was 'ultra-light weight.' This meant it was made of synthetic materials. I soon discovered that the slight slope of our tent site meant that, in the slippery sleeping bag, I slid downhill as I slept. I'd nod off, and then wake to find my feet pressed against the wall of the tent. I'd scrabble upward again and fall back asleep. Sleep, slide, scrabble, repeat.

I'm a middle-aged woman. I wake up for hot flashes. If I wake up in the night, I have to go to the bathroom or I'll never get back to sleep. Here on the mountainside, each trip involved scooching across the sandy tent floor, unzipping the tent flap in the dark, fumbling for boots, slipping them on and creeping out from under the rain fly, picking my way past tent lines across damp grass, down the steep, slippery path (where both Dad and I had each fallen on our respective butts at least once), tripping the motion sensor light, hunching shoulders against the unrelenting brightness of the bathroom fixtures, washing hands, trudging back through the obstacle course in the dark with light-dazzled eyes to unzip the tent, sit just inside the flap, take off boots and find a place to put them so I could easily find them for the next trip, then grope for the nylon-slickness of my sleeping bag, slide into it, caterpillar up the slope to my pillow, and nod off until the next thing woke me. Sometime in-between the sliding and scrabbling, I heard the rain begin to fall. Out I dashed to lower the window flaps so we wouldn't be soaked as we slept.

We were up before dawn, as were all the other pilgrims. Breakfast was once again sliced baguettes, butter, jam and coffee. The albergue staff had made up *bocadillas* (sandwiches) for pilgrims who had requested and paid the night before. Dad and I picked up our order and stuffed them in our packs. I stood outside chatting with Rick and Michael in the predawn darkness and they told me what an inspiration Dad was for them, not only was he mentally vital and engaged, he was vigorous and fit.

We all filled our water bottles and shouldered our packs. Then we were off, a long string of pilgrims on our way uphill again, dreaming of the moment when we found ourselves on the downward slope. Destination: Roncesvalles.

The sun was rising over the mountains to our left. I stopped to watch, and Carol and Ellen stopped too. Ellen and Dad chatted while Carol and I watched the sun rise and I read her John O'Donohue's "Blessing for a Traveler"[1] from my iPhone. She cried and thanked me.

Up, up, a gentler slope than yesterday, with strong winds keeping us cool. The Way out of Orisson begins as paved road winding through open fields across the beautiful and desolate treeless mountaintops. We passed herds of sheep grazing unfenced, beautiful vistas, and many landmarks.

I was full of coffee and, after an hour or so of walking, badly needed to pee. There are no cafés or places to answer the call of nature, and not a shrub or sheltering wall in sight. At last I could stand it no longer and told Dad that I was going to have to try out the poncho-as-shelter system. I left him and my pack on the road and, donning my poncho, stepped out into a large field.

When I had planned the porto-poncho scheme, I'd not taken into consideration the wind, which now was whipping and shifting from east, south, west, and back again. Unbuttoning, unzipping, and dropping-trou required both hands, how was I going to hold the poncho steady around my body and relax enough to actually pee? The ankle-length poncho cracked and snapped around me as I struggled to accomplish my goal without flashing any fellow pilgrims or soaking my socks. Fortunately, I completed my business before anyone walked by. Humility is an inevitable part of the pilgrim experience, and it doesn't hurt if one also has a healthy tolerance for the absurd. I kept my eyes on my feet as I trudged back to where Dad stood patiently waiting. He kindly refrained from comment. I shrugged out of the poncho, stuffed it back into my pack and we turned our faces to the next peak.

## Vierge D'Orisson

In only a few more steps we arrived at the "Vierge D'Orisson" (a wooden statue of the Virgin and child) that stands atop a rocky outcropping and overlooks the surrounding peaks.

The morning was overcast and the sun sent beams down through breaks in the clouds.

Here, I set down my pack and retrieved the small canister that contained Dusty's ashes. Again leaving my pack with Dad, I approached the shrine slowly, waiting for the pilgrim crouched at the foot of the statue to complete his devotion before I stepped forward. I placed the little metal box amongst the flowers, photos, kerchiefs and crosses that were strewn at the base of the Virgin's rocky perch. I bowed to take a photo for Joe and Candy and to say brief a prayer—hoping that by virtue of so many years of so many pilgrims' devotion, there was some of that Mysterious Otherness we understand as 'divine,' clinging to this windswept statue, and that it might benefit Dustin, his family and myself. I paused...wondering... then I gathered the canister up again and, carrying it in one hand, climbed to the top where the statue stood. I touched her briefly, and with another quick, wordless prayer, started back down, not wanting to prevent other pilgrims from taking their moment of contemplation.

Back at the curve in the path where Dad waited, I pushed the precious canister into its secret pocket, lifted the pack and, with a nod between us, Dad and I walked on.

The pavement wound ever upward. We passed shaggy horses roaming free and grazing, one wearing a belled collar that clanged soulfully in the cool wind. The cloud cover began to clear and the temperatures rose. We were grateful to come to an enterprising fellow with his white van by the side of the road, selling bananas, candy bars and sodas. He had a sign that read, "Buen Camino—The last French stamp," in several languages. Dad bought a candy bar. I chose a banana. We both bought Cokes. We also received stamps in our *credencials*[2] and answered the fellow's question about where we were from. He was keeping a daily tally of how many pilgrims passed by and whence they came. While we were there he was delighted to have his first pilgrim from Pakistan arrive and be counted.

Sitting to rest while we ate our snack, we visited with two women who were from Norway. Dad told them he had lived in Stavanger for a few years, they asked the inevitable question about his age, and we had a happy time marveling at his strength and vigor.

Further up and onward, the Camino left the pavement and headed up and over the pass towards Spain and our day's destination, Roncesvalles. We passed a stone carved with the news that we were 765 kilometers from "Saint Jacques de Compostelle"—as if we needed the reminder. We felt great to reach the top of the pass where we met a 37-year-old Brazilian who, upon learning Dad's age, grinned hugely and proclaimed himself ashamed of feeling tired in the presence of Harold. Then he asked if I would take a picture with his camera of him and Dad. The Norwegian ladies were there and wanted photos with him too. Celebrity Dad. Just beyond this crest, we filled our water bottles with ice-cold water at the Fountain of Roland and just beyond that, we crossed into Spain.

The border crossing is just a cattle guard. No one asks to see a passport; no visas are questioned or stamped. Once we were in Spain, the path was through woodlands. We were happy for the shade, but the path seemed to go on and up forever. At one point, we passed a small stone hovel and realized that had we tried to go beyond Orisson yesterday, this would have been the only shelter available before Roncesvalles. I kept wishing for the path to turn downhill.

We came to the end of the climb about 1 PM. We could see Roncesvalles far below us on the valley floor. We took a brief rest and then stepped onto the downward path.

The downhill stretch was covered in loose, round rocks varying from the size of grapes to the size of grapefruits.

It was so steep that people were shouting to one another to turn and walk sideways, like crabs scuttling down the hillside. Under the weight of our 20-lb. packs we were already fatigued, and the round, loose rubble beneath our boots shifted treacherously. A rock under Dad's foot rolled away as he put his weight on it. Dad caught his own balance back immediately, but his pack kept moving. I watched helplessly from a few steps above. He planted his walking stick and pressed hard against it to counter the shifting pack, but in excruciatingly slow motion, the pack dragged him off balance and carried him with it to the ground. He slammed onto the rocky path and began to roll, skidding to a stop a few feet further down the trail. Pilgrims rushed to help from all sides. One, a Spaniard, was exclaiming, "Did you see that fall? He dropped and rolled! That was a GREAT fall!" His admiration was evident and completely sincere. Many hands reached out, and Dad was literally lifted to his feet.

Other pilgrims collected Dad's pack and his walking stick. Concerned voices asked if he was injured or needed help. He brushed them off. He was completely unhurt except for having torn a tiny hole in one knee of his hiking pants. I was shaken by the fall almost as much as he, and we were both happy to sit down on a path-side log to let our adrenalin-induced dizziness wear off. Dad's fine metal hiking stick had bent under the strain of his struggle with gravity. He found a pair of fallen logs to wedge the stick between, and bent it back to nearly straight. I was beginning to see the wisdom of having two walking sticks rather than just one and I started looking around for something that might serve as a second staff for him. Though the path was littered with sticks and debris, nothing was long enough or strong enough to serve.

Having caught our breath, we slowly rose, brushed ourselves off and stepped once again onto the path. Rocks skittered under our boots and Dad fell two more times. This, for me, was the scariest part of the whole trip. Eventually, the rocks underfoot became a slightly more manageable path of embedded boulders. The strain on our knees was unbelievable on the steep downward grade. We became connoisseurs of rocky-steeps and began classifying various stretches as if they were rapids. The first stretch was Class 5 rapids. After that we were grateful to encounter Class 3 or under! At last the path entered a pine forest and we were walking on fairly smooth terrain.

It continued to be painfully steep and I began walking a 'serpentine' pattern, which increased the number of steps between me and Roncesvalles but gentled the slope and gave my knees a break. Our knees were so fatigued that, every once in a while, one of us would feel a leg buckle. We'd catch our balance, pause, and move on. We passed one fellow who had taken to walking backwards down the slope to ease his knees.

# Roncesvalles

About 4:30 PM we finally arrived in Roncesvalles. At the albergue, we were met by an official greeter—a volunteer who watched as we dropped to a nearby bench and removed our boots. He explained that we would need to go and make dinner reservations at one of the nearby restaurants, as the albergue did not provide food service. He impressed upon us that this was a priority because the dinner spots would fill up fast with so many pilgrims in town. We turned to the cashier to have our credencials stamped and pay for our stay. She asked our ages—54 and 82. She assigned us bed numbers. We had arrived so late that our beds were on the third floor. No elevator. As we stood at the register I spotted a pile of scallop shells painted with a red cross of St. James. Each shell had a long, red cord looped through a hole at the shell's base. I chose one and paid for it. Now I had a shell that I could tie on my pack; the little water bowl shell could stay safely tucked away with my watercolors. Funny how important to me it was to have that badge of identity. I was grateful I had found one so early in the trip.

I struggled up the stairs with my pack and was overjoyed to find that the sympathetic cashier had assigned both Dad and me to lower bunks. The midnight toilet visits would not have to include climbing ladders (or unzipping tents, for that matter). Beside each bunk was a cabinet where, for one Euro, one could lock one's belongings. I did not have a Euro coin and now had to face walking back down and up those stairs to get change. I stepped out into the walkway that ran along the foot of the row of bunks, calling to Dad that I was going to go downstairs for change. The despair in my heart must have echoed in my voice, because a wonderful Earth Mother named Peggy (from Seattle) stepped out to say that she had change. May there be eternal blessings upon Peggy, her children, and her children's children.

I returned to our cubby, handed Dad a Euro, used mine to lock up my pack, and I headed to the showers. After our showers, I left Dad to take a nap while I went off to make the dinner reservations. Out in the balmy evening, I walked across the vast courtyard and down a gentle slope to the corner where a couple of restaurants and hotels huddled together. I chose "La Posada" for our dinner place because I recognized it from the movie and thought Dad would get a kick out of eating there. I prepaid for our pilgrim dinners (9 Euro each), pocketed the ticket receipts, and made my slow way back up the slope, across the courtyard, and up the stairs to my bunk.

Pilgrim's dinner at La Posada is served in a large dining room at big, round tables. Among the folks at our table were Francesca (from Italy) who had been assigned the bunk above mine at our albergue, and Bill and Janice (from Calgary) who had been at Orisson the night before. We all caught up on our stories about the day's walk and agreed that sleeping tonight should be no problem at all. As the sun was setting, we stumbled off to bed.

# Notes

[1] O'Donohue, John. "For A Traveler." *To Bless The Space Between Us: A Book of Blessings.* New York: Doubleday, 2008. Print.

[2] Each pilgrim carries a "credencial," also known as a pilgrim passport. At each stop the pilgrim obtains a stamp from the local hostel, church, hotel, or café. Upon arriving in Santiago, the fully stamped credencial serves as proof that the pilgrim has indeed made the journey as claimed. At the Pilgrim Office in Santiago, if there are too few stamps, the pilgrim may find it difficult to obtain the Compostela (certificate of completion).

# CHAPTER 5

# Roncesvalles > Viskarret > Zubiri

T he lights were switched on at 6 AM. Hundreds of pilgrims blinking in the light began crawling out of bunks, pulling towels and socks from the bed frames (where they had hung to dry overnight) and stuffing them into packs. I joined the line to brush teeth and wash up.

There was no breakfast. The Roncesvalles albergue has a kitchen available to pilgrims who bring food to prepare. We had arrived too late and too weary to try and find a grocery or plan a morning meal. It was just as well. When we descended to the ground floor to put on our boots, we found the kitchen packed with pilgrims vying to use the microwaves and sinks. There were some vending machines with remarkably unappetizing snacks. Dad and I were ready to be away from the press of the crowd, so we passed on the gaudily packaged snacks and headed out into the dark morning. The glowing windows of the albergue lit our way as we crunched along the gravel path, past La Posada, and out of town.

Before long, we came to a small grocery store. I bought dates and granola bars, some bread and an orange. Dad and I convened at the picnic tables out front of the shop to fortify ourselves while the dawn sky grew brighter. Carol and Ellen came along and joined us. Carol asked me to read the "Blessing For a Traveler" again, and I did so. I also let her listen to David Whyte's reading of "Mameen"[1] which I had on my iPhone. More tears and gratitude. We chatted briefly and shared our food, then set out for today's destination, Zubiri.

The day was lovely and fresh. The first little town we passed through was Burgette (where Hemingway apparently stayed at times). There was a tiny café open for bustling business, serving *café con leche* (coffee with milk) and croissants to hungry pilgrims. Dad snagged us a table out front and I went in to get us each a cup of delicious coffee. I was grateful for the caffeine and was soon ready to get walking again.

The path was blessedly even and smooth. The guidebook warned that later in the day it would again become a steep descent, but—for the time being—it was a delight. The morning's coffee seemed to go through me quickly and I was soon looking for sheltering shrubbery. I was beginning to worry about the bathroom situation. I had brought with me a device designed to enable a woman to pee standing up—sort of a funnel-shaped thing called a pStyle, but I couldn't seem to convince my body to relax and let things flow when in a standing position. I figured I'd get used to it eventually and resigned myself to frequent, short nature breaks in the meantime.

We walked through woodlands, happy for the shade as the sun was beginning to beat down. We strolled down gentle slopes into a beautiful village of white-walled, red-roofed homes with splashy geraniums in every window.

## Viskarret

As the day grew warmer, the descent sharpened. I was beginning to long for a real, sit-down flushable toilet and was grateful to stop in Viskarret for lunch at the one café. Dad ordered a cool drink and pulled up a chair in the shade of a café umbrella while I went in to join the line of pilgrims waiting outside the restroom door. It was here, in a claustrophobically small WC in Viskarret that I realized my problem was more that just a need to sit down. The symptoms were familiar and undeniable. Three days and less than 25 miles into our 500 mile journey, I had developed a urinary tract infection. Hells bells.

I went out and sat next to Dad. As the other pilgrims had begun to wander away, I summoned the courage to tell him. He was great. He suggested that we ask the barista at the café to call us a taxi to drive us the final 10 km (~ six miles) to Zubiri. I wanted to tough it out and walk under my own steam, but we knew that the next stage of the trail was another long, steep descent. With the memory of yesterday's downhill juggernaut fresh in my mind, I agreed to the taxi.

The barista made the call for us and let us know that the one taxi in town was on another run at the moment but would be back for us in an hour. We waited happily, sitting in the sun on the benches in front of the café. I took advantage of the café's wifi and the iPhone's Skype app to call one of the hotels listed in the Camino de Santiago guidebook to make a reservation. I could not stay the night in a pilgrim hostel with lines for toilets and showers. I wanted an en suite bathroom with a hot shower—a place without the complications of sharing with ~25 other people.

While we were waiting, another (younger) father and daughter pair of pilgrims wandered up. They were planning to stay overnight in Viskarret having walked the full St. Jean to Roncesvalles trek the day before. When they heard we had a taxi coming, they asked if they could share a ride part of the way. They needed to get to the next town because there was no ATM in Viskarret and they were going to need more funds before they could pay their B&B and start their walk again. We were glad to share the ride and, when the taxi arrived, were delighted to find it was a small van, so there was plenty of room for all of us.

As we rode down the hill I became more and more glad that we had not chosen to try and walk. The number of switchbacks and the vistas that opened along the side of the winding road testified to the rugged steep that would have been our trail if we were on foot.

# Zubiri

The driver dropped us at the door of Hosteria Zubiri. Beware false cognates. "*Hosteria*" is not a hostel—it is an "inn." This was a lovely one. It was cool inside and welcoming. The very nice lady at the front desk gave me directions to the *farmacia*, and Dad checked us in. Our room was only one flight up and the bathroom had both a shower and a tub. Heaven.

In Spain, the pharmacies are staffed with the equivalent of nurse practitioners. They can assist with diagnosis and dispense some medicines. We had arrived in town just before *siesta* time. Every Spanish town shuts down completely from about 2:30 to 7:30 PM for siesta. If I was going to see someone about my problem, I needed to hurry.

I found the farmacia as directed, several blocks away, and arrived just minutes before the posted siesta closing time. I was relieved to find that the woman there spoke very good English. She could not give me antibiotics—I'd have to see a doctor for that—but she asked me questions about the severity of my symptoms and we agreed that I would probably be okay with a couple of weeks worth of cranberry capsules and lots of water. She also advised me not to sit on stone or metal seats. I figured I could try to sit only on wooden chairs and benches or the ground. Ritual is part of the pilgrim experience.

No more orange juice, café con leche, or wine—water only until this UTI cleared up. Okay. Self-denial is part of the pilgrim experience.

Back to the hotel I went, glad in my heart that once I got there I would be able to take off my boots and put my feet up for HOURS. Dad and I washed our clothes and hung them to dry on the hotel terrace. I took two baths. I noticed what looked like blood blisters forming around my swollen ankles and calves. I figured they were caused by the tight elastic of my hiking socks and decided to fold the socks over the top of my boots from then on.

We both napped—it was, after all, siesta time. We spent some time sorting and repacking our packs. Dad went out and found an ATM and a *supermercado*. We agreed that I'd be more likely to have a speedy recovery if I took it easy for a couple of days. Our plan was to take a taxi to Pamplona then stay there for a rest day. Dad had struck up a friendship with the lady at the front desk (I told you) and found that there was a bus we could take to Pamplona in the morning. She was able to recommend a hotel in Pamplona, and she even called to make our reservation for us.

Once siesta was over, Dad and I walked up the street and found a place advertising a Pilgrim Menu. We seated ourselves at a long table and did our best to decipher the menu. Once we had ordered, other pilgrims arrived and reported that the afternoon's descent had been harder than the one into Roncesvalles. Both Dad and I were glad to have confirmation that we'd made the right decision with the taxi.

The food was pretty awful—greasy pork steaks, french fries, olive and mayonnaise salad, with not a lettuce leaf in sight. It mattered very little. We were tired and we were hungry. We ate and paid as quickly as we could and were back in our room before sundown.

We retrieved our clothes, dried already in the hot sun. I took one more shower, just because I could. I posted a blog for the folks back home with only the slightest mention of my health problems and with absolutely NO mention of the falling. The blog was to reassure those at home, not to worry them. At last, all chores done, we turned out the lights and slept.

# Notes

[1] Whyte, David. "Mameen." Orch. Jeff Rona. *David Whyte: Return*. Many Rivers, 2011. CD.

# CHAPTER 6

# Pamplona

We were out at the bus stop early in the morning. The bus is apparently the daily commuter bus for folks who need to get to Pamplona for work. We met a pair of French pilgrims on the bus who also were planning a day of rest in Pamplona. We parted from them at the taxi stand outside Pamplona's central bus station and hopped into a cab that took us to the Hotel Eslava where we were staying. Dad had intentionally booked us into a place on the extreme west side of Pamplona within a block of the Camino so we would not have to walk through the entire city the next morning when we left.

During our planning for the Camino, neither of us had anticipated a day of rest so early in the pilgrimage, so we were woefully uninformed about the sights. We asked at the front desk for a map and were told that all the English-language tourist maps were gone. I chose a French one, Dad chose a Spanish-language one, and we set out to see what we could see. Very near to our hotel was the Cathedral San Lorenzo. We took a quick peek inside, pausing to watch as the morning mass concluded. Emerging back into the overcast day, we wandered into the central part of the city looking for the Plaza de Castillo. This is the main plaza and is a tourist destination mainly because it is where one finds Café Iruña—famously a favorite haunt of Hemingway. We decided to have lunch under the arches out in front of the café. Pamplona is the place on the Camino where the Hemingway fascination is strongest. I find Hemingway an intriguing character, but his connection to Spain was not mine. He was a pilgrim of a different sort, and the constant "Hemingway slept here" drumbeat seemed like something that would have caused him a good deal of irritation.

After our lunch, too weary and 'pilgrim-brained' to be able to figure out sightseeing or read our French/Spanish maps, we just followed our noses around random corners and down narrow streets. I say 'pilgrim-brained' because I was beginning to notice an odd sense of removal, a mental distance from the city rhythms and the glut of words crammed into our maps and guidebooks in tiny, nine-point type.

Only three days into our walk, the roles and responsibilities of my 'real life' were dropping away, and with my physical health issues filling a good part of my awareness, I found myself unable to engage in the strategic decision-making process that would have happened in a flash back home. It was a state of mind not unlike the stunned stillness that happens when one is first plunged into grief. I felt unable to focus on questions like, "Should we see the cathedral or the museum?" and "If the cathedral is going to close in two hours, is it worth the admission price, or should we go elsewhere?" I think Dad was experiencing something similar, because whenever these questions arose between us, we'd pause, look at one another—

hoping the other would have an answer—and then just shrug and walk on, deciding not to decide.

I told Dad that I wanted to find a coin purse to manage all the loose change that kept accumulating in my pockets, so we began strolling from shop to shop, looking in windows, glancing down alleyways, and soaking in Pamplona's ancient presence. I tried a few zippered pouches, but they tended to catch on folded paper money making them too difficult to open and close. Drawstring bags didn't open wide enough or stay open long enough to accommodate my painfully slow counting out of unfamiliar coins and bills. Most coin purses on offer were covered with bulky ornamentation that caused them to snag going in and out of my pockets.

Dad was the picture of patience, helping me scour shop windows and interiors. I thought he must be bored out of his gourd. (Purse shopping cannot have been his idea of a great use of our day in Pamplona.) But he seemed to prefer accompanying me on my obsessive quest to splitting up and going on separate adventures. At last I found a simple little red leather envelope-shaped pouch with a squeeze-frame closure. It was big enough to hold a day's worth of coins and bills and small enough to slide easily in and out of the cargo pocket on my hiking pants, and it would open with a squeeze and pop closed as soon as I released pressure. Perfect. I paid the nice lady and immediately transferred my money to my little treasure and buttoned it safely into its pocket-home.

Siesta time was looming, so we headed back to our hotel. As we neared the hotel, we noticed a sporting goods store just a few doors down. It was already closed for siesta. We agreed to come back later when it reopened after National Naptime and see whether they had a water bottle that would suit Dad's needs.

On the trail, he had been carrying two, half-liter plastic soda bottles filled with water—keeping one in each side pocket of his pack. I carried a single liter-sized bottle on my pack and a much smaller canteen-like water bottle in one of my pants cargo pockets. When Dad wanted to have a drink on the trail, he needed me to reach one of his bottles and put it back for him. When I wanted a drink, I could pull the mini-canteen out of my pocket and take a sip without breaking stride. He was hoping to find a durable little bottle like mine.

We retreated to the hotel room and napped for a short while. Then we puttered around the room performing our now daily ritual of unpacking, sorting, reorganizing and re-packing our packs. Dad kept up a cheery stream of chatter, and I responded with inarticulate grunts and groans as I was suffering with a pounding, caffeine-withdrawal headache. I finally begged him to let me have some time alone in the room.

Once again, he was a hero. He said, "Your mom needs a lot of time to herself too," then he picked up his daypack and windbreaker and set out to wander Pamplona on his own and see if he could find a good place for us to have dinner. I laid down for a few minutes of meditation then pulled out the little parcel that held my Camino journal and paint kit. To the sound of Hildegarde von Bingen chants playing on my phone's iTunes app, I spent a restorative hour-and-a-half, relaxing my shoulders, writing in my tiny journal, and painting a small watercolor from one of the photos I'd taken the day before. Dad returned to a much more civilized daughter.

As it came to the end of siesta time, we ventured out again and went straight to the sporting goods store. They did not have a water bottle that would work, but they did have walking sticks. Knowing that we had many more steep and rocky descents in our future, Dad and I agreed to buy a pair of walking sticks and then each take one. We'd each be walking with a mismatched pair, but that didn't matter. A person's two walking sticks need only match in length. The sticks we already had were fully adjustable, as was the new pair. So what if the colors and styles were eclectic? Letting go of vanity is part of the pilgrim experience.

Rather than pay for another restaurant dinner, we decided to drop into a local grocery where we bought bread, apples, bananas, and oranges. We didn't know we were supposed to weigh the produce and generate a pricing label before taking it to the cashier. Our ignorance caused a minor rush hour traffic jam in the little shop while the cashier first tried to explain what we should do with our fruit (we didn't understand his Spanish) and then took the produce back across the store to weigh it for the *Americanos estupidos*. Chastened and chuckling, we left with our bounty and ate sitting on a bench in a big park near our hotel.

## Linda's Journal

*September 12 –*
*I think it's Wednesday. I feel that I may be cramping Dad's style with my mini health crisis, but he insists not. We wandered around Pamplona and then came back to our hotel for siesta. I took a long nap, still pounding with a caffeine headache because NO COFFEE while I recover from a mild UTI. I'm doing MUCH better today and the major issue now is drippy nose and headache.*

*I'm hoping to wake tomorrow a new woman—I'll need to be—Class 5 rocky descent near the mid-to-end of day tomorrow. Dad & I stopped at a nearby sporting goods store and bought a set of walking sticks to share (one each) so we'll both have 2 sticks for the coming day's challenge. Once again, we've each repacked and reorganized our packs, leaving a few things in the closet here for someone else who may need them.*

# CHAPTER 7

# Pamplona > Puente la Reina

## Blog Entry — September 13, 2012

We woke at 5:30 AM and were checked out of the hotel and tapping along the sidewalks with our new walking sticks by 6:30 AM. It was still dark, so we followed the Camino out of town by spotting the metal medallions embedded in the sidewalks, bearing the sign of the scallop shell and gleaming under the still glowing street lamps.

The way out of Pamplona runs through the little bedroom community of Cizur Menor along a main road. In the drizzly predawn darkness, truck headlights illuminated spray from massive, fast-moving tires as they barreled past us. Everyone seemed to be going to Pamplona rather than leaving. The oncoming headlights blinded us and compounded the difficulty of seeing the way forward. The yellow arrows (trail markers that all pilgrims rely on to point the way) were nowhere to be found. Had we taken a wrong turn in the dark? Or was it just that our little headlamps were not strong enough to pick out yellow arrows painted on random signposts or roadside signage? Were we on the wrong side of the road? Had the path turned from the main road at some invisible juncture? We stopped and conferred with another pilgrim who was also beginning to worry about the lack of yellow arrows. We finally spotted one on a wooden post and set out again, grateful to see color returning to the world as the sun began to rise.

After we left the city behind, the day's climb began. In the distance, we could see a line of wind turbines along a ridge. The drizzle became a light rain. We kept climbing, the gravelly grade becoming steeper as the rain came and went. Sun would break through for a few moments, then the rain would move in on the next wind. As we emerged from a sheltered lane, the vista opened up and we could just see the beginning of a rainbow. I am a connoisseur of Rainbow Weather, so I knew to stop and watch. Other booted pilgrims crunched past us as Dad and I stood there, watching the rainbow's colors grow stronger and develop into a full glowing arch.

---

The trail grew rockier, and Dad and I were celebrating our new walking sticks. Having two sticks each improved our balance and shifted some of the load off our knees on the steeps. We were climbing up to the ridge with the windmills and (as you might expect) the wind picked up and kept us cool.

I was determined to redeem myself after my snail's pace climbing the Pyrenees, so I leant into the slope and kept my feet moving. One step at a time. "Damned metaphors," I muttered to myself. The Camino experience is jam-packed with them.

## Alto del Perdón

We arrived at the peak and I gratefully shed my pack and sat at the base of the monument there, eating a bit of a snack and gazing around at the view and the crowds. The peak is a destination spot for pilgrims and day-trippers alike. It is called 'the hill of pardon' because in earlier days, pilgrims who reached the top of this peak but were unable to go on, were given a pardon from finishing and granted their *Compostela* (certificate of completion of the pilgrimage).

While we were standing on the peak—taking turns with other pilgrims posing for photos by the sculpture there (a metal silhouette of a line of pilgrims)—more pilgrims arrived, rushing up from below with the news that a woman had broken a leg on the trail. Other pilgrims had the necessary phones and language skills to call for help.

Later, at the albergue in Puente la Reina, we learned from another pilgrim (a doctor who was at the peak at the time) that the EMTs arrived about 15 minutes later. Apparently, the injured pilgrim was an elderly lady who attempted the walk without being really fit. The stones on the path were slippery in the drizzle, and anyone could have fallen, but her age and lack of conditioning meant that her tumble was the end of her journey. I hoped that having made it to the Alto del Perdón, she would award herself her own Compostela for bravery and effort. If I had met her, I would have given her a pardon myself.

It was time to start our descent into Puente la Reina. Dad and I stood up and performed what I had come to call our Pilgrim Macarena, patting shirt pockets, hip pockets, and cargo pockets near the knees ending with a quick spin to scan the area and confirm that passport, wallet, credencial, canteen, walking sticks and sunglasses were not being left behind. With everything in place and new walking sticks in hand, we crossed the road that ran along the ridge of the peak and headed downhill—very cautiously. This descent, we decided, was a mere Class 4. It only lasted about mile and a half. Then we had relatively level going all the way into Puente la Reina.

# Puente la Reina

For all my attempts at redemption, I was still a pokey pilgrim. The weight of the pack and the severity of the inclines were playing havoc with my land speed. Dad had begun walking behind me, because if he walked in front, he soon left me behind. His strength was amazing, as was his patient willingness to go at my pace. We arrived at Puente la Reina about 4 PM, nearly ten hours after we started out.

We stopped at the first albergue only to find that the last bed had just been taken. We pulled out the guidebook and saw that there was a brand new albergue on the far side of town. Hoping that there would be beds for us when we arrived, we set out, trying to stay ahead of the pilgrims coming up from behind. We pushed on as fast as I could go through the charming old town and across the famous bridge from which the town gets its name.

We reached the edge of town and found a sign indicating that the albergue we sought, while out of sight around a bend, was nearby—at the top of a very steep hill. I was lagging, and the long line of pilgrims who were also questing for resting places was about to overtake us. Try as I might, I could go no faster up the white gravel hill and within two minutes found myself watching as Dad passed me by, leaving me in his dust (literally). He trekked upwards and out of my sight around the curve, as if the day's hike was just beginning. When I dragged myself to the door of the albergue fifteen minutes later, a grinning German couple sitting at a picnic table there informed me, "Your fasser hass already arrieft." Humility is part of the pilgrim experience.

The albergue was a vast building with several multi-bunk rooms, a café/bar with dining room, coin-op laundry machines, shiny new shower facilities, a pool, and picnic area. Dad was waiting for me at the long bar in the dining room where a gruff fellow stamped our credencials with barely a word. He asked whether we wanted to pay for the pilgrim meal that would be served in the dining room later. I thought about that hill and the long walk back into town and said I would definitely be eating here. I could not imagine retracing my steps, having managed to get this far. Having purchased both dinner and breakfast meals, we wandered off to find bunks and showers.

There were several rooms with multiple bunks and we chose one where we could each have a lower bunk. We had passed a pair of laundry machines on our way to the bunk-rooms and were eager to take advantage of them, but showers, as always, were the first order of business.

The shower rooms were wonderfully new and modern with white tiles shining in the late afternoon light, but they lacked shelves or chairs so it was a challenge to keep my clean clothes dry while I showered and toweled off. The shower stalls were open to the dressing room area, covered only by short curtains that did nothing to prevent water from running across the floor of the entire room. Juggling clothes and towel to keep them above the growing puddles, I finished my shower and then performed the one-foot-at-a-time balancing act of dressing. As I stepped to the sink to comb my wet hair, a pilgrim I'd never seen before came in for her turn at the showers and stopped to ask me if I was Linda. Wondering why she wanted to know, I said I was, to which she replied, "I've heard a lot about you. You and your father are famous on the Camino." Right. Famous Dad—Pilgrim Legend!

Back in the bunkroom, gathering up my and Dad's clothes for laundry, I found familiar faces, fresh from their showers, doing the same. I joined Elmarie (from Australia) and Louise (from Ireland) to investigate the washer and dryer situation. The price of a wash was 5 Euro! It would take another 5 Euro to dry a load. Louise looked crestfallen. That sort of expense was well out of a typical pilgrim's budget. I looked at the large capacity of the machines and suggested that we all combine our laundry into a single load and split the cost. Perfect.

I went back to the café/bar and purchased a package of laundry detergent containing two large biscuit-shaped cakes of dry soap. Our impromptu laundry committee collected everyone's laundry and Louise served as treasurer, accepting Euro coins from each of us. I was mystified by the machinery, unable to work out how to insert the coins, where to put the soap, and how to start the washer. Louise had much better luck and soon our clothes were soaking and swishing in hot water.

Some of the others had gone out to have a dip in the pool. I wandered over to check it out, but a pretty cool breeze was kicking up and the water was unheated. I sat on the edge and soaked my weary feet. My lower legs were now covered with an angry-looking red rash. They also were swollen, apparently from water retention. Shivering in the dropping temperatures, I wandered back inside. Dad was having a nap so I joined Louise and her pals from Ireland out at a little grouping of picnic tables that sat near a laundry drying line. I was wearing shorts, and the state of my lower legs became a topic of group discussion. I put my feet up on a bench, hoping to relieve the swelling. One of the young women pulled a tube of

Arnica out of her bag, squeezed a portion out onto her hands and began massaging it into my calves and feet. I could not believe the kindness and care I was receiving from a total stranger. This is the way it is on the Camino. Each pilgrim is every pilgrim. We do what we can to help, encourage and support one another on the journey.

The dinner bell rang and those of us who had chosen to stay at the albergue for dinner filed into the dining room and took places at a long row of tables. It was a fairly typical pilgrim meal—roast chicken or fried pork, french-fried potatoes, red table wine and bottled water. We laughed and exchanged stories, learning where each one at the table had begun their walk, where they were from, and how far they were planning to go. Some pilgrims take the Camino in stages. Many pilgrims we met were only able to get one or two weeks away from their work, so they were walking as far as they could in that amount of time, planning to return later to pick up wherever they left off. Others were between jobs, taking the rare opportunity of having several weeks free to walk the full distance.

Louise and her friends had chosen to take dinner in town, so they weren't at the long table with us. They must have delayed their trip into town because when Dad and I got back to our bunks, we found our clothes clean, dried, and neatly folded. We felt so cared for. This is how it is on the Camino. Pilgrims are the source and receivers of great kindness.

## Harold's Journal

Day 8. September 13, 2012

We were up at 5:45 and on the Camino by 6:30. The climb up to Alto de Perdón was grim. It was cold with a light rain that caused the steep, boulder-filled path to be very slick. The path was primarily black clay. We arrived at the top of the Alto de Perdón at noon. An elderly woman had fallen and broken her leg behind us. Spanish-speaking pilgrims called for emergency assistance that arrived in about 15 minutes. The steep down-hill was not as bad as the way to Roncesvalles. We walked all the way to Puente la Reina. We arrived at 4:30 in the afternoon and we stayed in the clean, new Albergue Santiago Apostoli. Both Linda and I got lower bunks. They have washers and dryers so now we have all clean clothes. We ate at the albergue and met numerous wonderful people.

# CHAPTER 8

# Puente la Reina >
# Estella > Los Arcos

Pilgrim rhythm was establishing itself in our days. An early rise—about 6 AM—breakfast (if offered) and then on the road as the sun was rising. "Breakfast" in the Albergue Santiago Apostoli was coffee, orange juice, and bread with prepackaged butter and jam. I was feeling better, so I decided to have a cup of café con leche. Such is the power of the caffeine addiction.

We were now on our seventh day of walking. Like every other pilgrim we'd met, we were following John Brierley's guidebook, and today's assignment was a 14-mile trek from Puente la Reina to Estella. This would be the longest day yet.

We left Puente la Reina, with a brief backward glance at the Romanesque bridge that gives the town its name. The bridge was built on the queen's command in medieval times to allow pilgrims safe passage.

I snapped a photo of the still-sleeping village at dawn and then we set out for Estella. The path was hilly but rarely steep, and at many times we found ourselves walking on the old Roman-built road or crossing a Roman bridge.

Those Romans built things to last. In most places, what we were really walking on was the 'sub-road'—a layer of rubble the road builders tamped into the ground over which they laid the now-missing paving stones. Apparently the sub-layer was designed to allow water to drain away so the overlaid paved road would stay dry and mud-free. The surviving sub-road consists of largish round rocks firmly embedded in the dirt path. I christened it "the Roman foot massage" because each stone you step on digs like a rounded fist deep into the sole of your boot. The walking sticks were proving their worth on this uneven surface by minimizing stumbling and ankle-twisting.

# Lorca

Another revelation was that steep paths were not limited to the distances between towns. Many towns sit on hillsides or crests. We were learning that you don't just pass through a Spanish town, you climb the town. The town of Lorca, about 7.5 miles into the day's walk, is a prime example. The town is so steep that the sidewalks are more like staircases.

Having climbed to a café, we joined a busy buzz of Pilgrims all taking a quick break for refreshments, wifi and flushable toilets. We sat with David (from San Diego) and Tina (from Philadelphia) and chatted, then pulled ourselves to our feet again and continued onward and upward.

As we crossed through the town square on our way out of town, we passed a gathering crowd of people wearing matching T-shirts and carrying musical instruments. A stage was set up in the square and they appeared to be preparing for a town fiesta. Following the yellow arrows and scallop shells marking the way, we turned a corner into a tiny street. At the same time, we heard the band strike up in the square we'd just left. We could hear them getting louder and realized that they were marching in our direction. Dad and I ducked into an alley to let them pass, then we marched along behind them until their path and ours diverged.

We paused at the foot of a Roman bridge to eat our bocadillas (bought at a café early in the morning) for lunch. My feet were so hot in my boots, I took them off and put on my sandals. I didn't walk far before I was ready to switch back. The Roman Foot Massage was too much for my soft Keene sandals. The miles and heat were really beginning to weigh, and I was moving more and more slowly as we made our weary way into Estella.

# Estella

Once again, the end of day ritual of finding a bed required an uphill climb. The albergues at the foot of the hill were already full and when we finally located the Albergue Perroquiel, we joined a long line of weary pilgrims waiting for a chance at a bed. We were fortunate to get two of the last available bunks that night. A few minutes after we collapsed on our bunks, a pilgrim came in with a mattress to put on the floor as there were no more beds in the albergue.

## Linda's Journal

*September 14 –*

*Another 14 mile day and at the end, my feet were killing me. We were among the last ones to find places in the albergue in Estella. It is extremely basic...absolutely no frills. There is one shower and 2 toilets for women. (Dad says there's only one shower and one toilet for the men.) Beds are bunks in 2 rooms (co-ed). Mattresses covered in plastic. My UTI is bothering me a bit today. Probably my own fault for having juice and coffee this morning. I'll not do that again. Tomorrow is another tough hike—and Dad and I have made a reservation at Hotel Monaco in Los Arcos (tomorrow's destination). We've agreed to take a taxi and skip the next day. Temps are predicted to be very hot and the walk looks dangerously difficult. I've been to the farmacia again and have bought cortisone cream for my legs which have an angry red rash on the shins and calves. Apparently, it is a reaction to sweat inside my clothes (diaper rash, essentially).*

*Today I realized that—to some extent—I've been doing the Pilgrimage with other people's expectations and plans in mind. I've been struggling to match the other pilgrims' schedule and to keep up (not slow Dad down) for Dad's sake, and that is a lesson for me. I do much of my life that way. This walk asks—demands—to be done on one's own terms or not at all, so I'll walk, and remember what happens to my health when I deny my own reality and try to match or please another's.*

*I admit to myself that I'm worried about tomorrow's trek. I hope I feel better in my UTI. It is enough to deal with feet and shoulders.*

---

We went downhill to find an evening meal, but had to wait for the cafés to open. Americans and weary pilgrims are ready for a meal by 5 PM but in Spain, siesta is not over until nearly 7 PM. That is the earliest one can expect to find a meal. While we waited, we made the acquaintance of two more Pilgrims: Lena (from Denmark) and a friend of hers. Lena was planning to walk all the way to Santiago. Her friend was there for only one or two weeks then would be heading back home.

We ate the 'Pilgrim Menu' (salad or pasta to start, choice of fish, pork, or chicken with french fries as second course, and yogurt, fruit salad, or ice cream to finish), then wobbled on sore feet back up the hill to bed.

Back at the albergue, the lights were not out yet, but Dad and I hit the hay. Even with my special dental appliance, my sleep apnea causes me to snore sometimes. This usually happens when I first fall asleep and am really tired. I must have been snoring on this occasion because I was woken by my bed being strongly shaken. A trio of young people from Israel were standing in the space between the bunks, having a conversation and, apparently, I'd disturbed them. I hoped they would be sound sleepers. I did not want to be shaken awake all night long.

As it turned out, they didn't shake me awake later, but I can't say the same for the unfortunate soul in the lower bunk to my left. In the middle of the night, the young woman in the bed above mine climbed out of her bed and into the top bunk to my left with one of her comrades. The energy of youth. Amazing.

## Los Arcos

Up at 5 AM, packing in the dark because other pilgrims were still asleep. Once again, a quick breakfast of bread, butter and jam then out into the dark streets following other pilgrims with sticks tapping along the cobblestones. We saw light spilling into the street from a *panaderia* (bakery) and stopped to buy the day's bocadillas. We'd been warned that there would be no place to get food along the walk from Estella to Los Arcos. Dad slung our sandwiches from a bag attached to his pack, and we were off again by 7:30.

At about 8 AM we passed the Monastario Irache where they have a fountain that offers pilgrims a choice between water and red wine. It was a bit early for wine, and both Dad and I had full water bottles, so we just paused to watch other pilgrims taking photos of one another sampling the wine. The day was already warm, so we didn't linger long.

The trek to Los Arcos was the gentlest slope and least rocky we'd had so far. The second half of the 14-mile day, however, was completely without shade and without passing through any towns. The day's heat broke records and there was no breath of a breeze. We walked across the flat, scorched landscape feeling the sun's hot hammer pounding us with every step. At midday, we were searching for some source of shade where we could sit and eat our lunch. I was also hoping to find shelter for a 'nature break.' A towering stack of hay bales was the only possibility in sight, and we could see for miles. As we came even with the haystack, we saw that other pilgrims—three Frenchmen as it turned out—were there having their snack in its shade. Dad and I joined them, putting down our packs on the stubble of the field.

I circled the stack and realized that there was no place where I'd be out of sight of either the road or my fellow pilgrims, so I hiked out into the middle of the field where there was a small mountain of chicken poop. I'm guessing it was intended to be spread as fertilizer eventually, but in that moment it was the only option for a 'toilet.' The filth was appalling. I used my two walking sticks to brace myself so I wouldn't accidentally touch any of the manure as I squatted and took care of business as quickly as possible. Back in the shade of the hay, I used some of Dad's hand sanitizer and then ate, holding my sandwich with the wrapper between my hands and the bread. Pilgrimage is not elegant. Filth and endurance are part of the pilgrim experience.

We soldiered on and actually made pretty good time, arriving at the edge of Los Arcos at about 2:30 PM. Walking into a Spanish town midafternoon feels like an old western film. The streets are deserted. All is silent except for the sound of the wind. Dust devils kicking up are the only movement one sees. We were parched from the long walk across the sun's anvil and were greatly relieved to find a small shaded alcove at the very edge of town. There were benches to rest on and vending machines with ice cold drinks. Dad had a Coke and I had water. Cool, clear water.

After the last two days' push to find beds, we had decided to book into a hotel in Los Arcos. Hotel Monaco was on the opposite side of town, and we were so tired and bedraggled by the time we arrived, the receptionist just gave us the key to our room and told us to go on up. She would check us in after we'd showered and rested. I remain deeply grateful for her compassion in that moment.

I had a shower, and then Dad had his. We checked in and I went back up to the room to soak in a bath. Dad went out to explore the town. I could not have walked another step, but he had energy to go out. After my soak, a little bed rest and a round of pack reorganization, I too made my way to the town square where I found Dad sitting at a café table under an umbrella surrounded by six or seven other pilgrims. Peggy was there, my friend from Roncesvalles who had the Euro for the locker, along with her husband Steve. Evelyn from Ireland (who had recently undergone heart surgery), Elmarie from

Australia, David from San Diego and Tina from Philadelphia were all there too. The table was laden with pitchers of sangria and plates of snacks. Sadly, there was to be no sangria for me. I was back on my no-caffeine-no-alcohol regimen having sincerely regretted the coffee of the day before.

Eventually the party split up as people headed back to their albergues to freshen up before dinner. Evelyn decided to join Dad and me for dinner. We chose to eat at the Hotel Monaco. We walked into the dining room and soon found ourselves in an episode of *Fawltey Towers*. We were given menus and glasses of water. After a brief wait, the waiter arrived at our table to announce loudly, "There is problema en cocina. Only no chicken."

Confusion reigned for nearly ten minutes while Dad, Evelyn and I tried to communicate with this ranting Spaniard and his resignedly calm female coworker, his voice growing ever louder and more emphatic, she kneeling between me and Evelyn trying to whisper and point at menu items to confirm whether they were available and WHAT exactly they contained. In the end, we each managed to order and then just sat and laughed until tears were streaming. Meal accomplished, Dad and I turned in and slept well.

The next day was Sunday. The forecast was for temperatures in the 90's and the trail was reported to have two very steep and treacherous descents with no place for shade or water, so we decided to travel this section to Logroño by bus. We'd have another night in a hotel there then set out on foot again on Monday morning.

While in Los Arcos, I sat down with John Brierley's guidebook to review his plans for the next few days' walking. It was finally sinking in that I was not going to be able to continue covering the 15 to 20 miles-per-day he recommended. What was also dawning, was the realization that we didn't have to stick to the guidebook's schedule. If I was going to make it to Santiago, some adjustments to the plan would need to be made. I broached the subject with Dad, and he agreed that we might be better off planning to walk no more than 15 km a day (about 9 miles). I hoped that I could go easy for a couple of weeks, recover my health and build my strength. Maybe later in the walk we could begin ramping up the distances again. As usual, Dad was totally willing to shift the plan, and I was grateful. Flexibility is part of the pilgrim experience.

## Linda's Journal

*September 15 –*
*We have walked 14 miles today carrying our packs and are now in a hotel room in Los Arcos...and we plan to take the bus tomorrow to Logroño and another hotel room...I hope to feel recovered from the UTI which seems to be trying to flare again.*

*Loss of control...losing control...I can't know what my body will do next...swelled ankles and legs...UTI...I don't know how to inhabit this body. I want to walk shorter distances. I want to carry less load. I want to be on Camino and not in hospital.*

*I need to pack...reassess everything in my pack and reorganize how I pack it because (a) it is too heavy and (b) the current system means I can't pack the night before if I've had the sleeping bag out.*
*1. plastic bag for sleeping bag and tie it outside pack, or*
*2. put it in last and resign myself to 'heavy on top'...or...?*

*Once again, tired, in pain, unsure of my health, hesitant to speak up about it...looking for the lessons...everything on the Camino is a metaphor.*

---

## Harold's Journal

Day 10. September 15, 2012

We walked 13.1 miles today from Estella to Los Arcos. Temperature was in the 80's today and really hot while we were walking. We had one hill but finished it at midday. It was about halfway to Los Arcos. We started walking about 7:15 in the morning and arrived in Los Arcos about 2:15 in the afternoon. We made really good time. We checked into the Hotel Monaco. We had a great room with an overhead fan, good shower and tub so we both cleaned up and went to the Plaza where many of our Pilgrim friends were collecting. Had good talks with several of our friends. Called Veranne and talked to her. There were a lot of pilgrims in this hotel tonight. We will eat a pilgrim menu tonight, probably in our hotel. We don't know if other pilgrims will join us or not. Tomorrow we're going to take the day off. It is forecast to be in the high 90s and the Camino has two dangerous down slopes. We will take the bus to Logroño and spend the night in a hotel.

---

# CHAPTER 9

# Logroño > Navarette

We met the French couple again on the bus ride to Logroño and discovered we were all booked into the same hotel, so we shared a taxi from the bus station to the hotel. We were disappointed to discover that our hotel had no laundry service on Sundays. Ah, the trials of pilgrimage. Laundry had to wait.

This Sunday, Logroño was celebrating the Festival of San Mateo. A large section of the city streets had become a pedestrian mall with street performers attracting wide circles of crowding audiences, and local clubs and guilds marching in groups carrying banners and announcing their affiliation by wearing matching T-shirts and bandanas. One plaza was set up with massive tents under which food was being cooked up and sold. Huge deep fryers yielded all manner of mysterious breaded treats, but it was so hot that neither Dad nor I could imagine eating a hot, greasy meal. Instead, we wandered in the crowd until we found a small storefront place that sold Greek food. We sat at a table out in the plaza and ate baked chicken and salad (me), and a Gyro sandwich and the ubiquitous fries (Dad). A young couple sat next to us and asked where we'd found our meal. They were pilgrims too and—as always—amazed to discover Dad was a fellow peregrino.

As Dad and I made our way back to the hotel, we encountered a column of horse-drawn carriages apparently making their way to join a gathering point for a parade.[1]

We made it an early night and were happy that our room was at the back of the hotel, away from the boisterous celebrations in the streets below.

We wound our way out of Logroño at 7:15 Monday morning. It was tricky because it was not as well marked as other cities and towns. We found the way in spite of ample opportunity for confusion and lengthened our strides as we walked through parkland around the edge of a lake.

As we left the park we came to open country covered with vineyards. It was harvest time and we stopped to watch a load of freshly picked grapes being carried by forklift to the end of a row and set down on the red earth. A pair of Korean pilgrims also stopped to take a picture. The driver of the lift saw us and indicated that we could have some. We all hesitated, unsure we'd understood his gesture correctly. He waved us towards the grapes again and opened the window of his cab to shout, "*Buen Camino!*" Beautiful, juicy grapes, just picked, their flavor foreshadowing the wine they'll be used to make = a perfect midmorning snack.

## Navarette

As we came to the outskirts of Navarette, we passed the ruins of a pilgrim hostel built in the 1100's. Passing it slowly, on weary feet, looking at the outlines of the ancient entryway and rooms, gave a sense of how many pilgrims over the centuries have walked and rested together along the Camino. We arrived at our albergue by 11:00 AM having walked our newly agreed distance of nine miles. It was a new one that opened in 2010 and felt like luxury accommodations with bunks tall enough so those on lower bunks could sit up in bed! We took showers and did laundry in the washroom on the second floor (I wrung water out of the clothes while Dad leant out the window to hang them on the line strung along the outer wall of the building). Chores done, we spotted the church bell tower and headed in that direction knowing that the square (and center of activity) would be nearby. We arrived at the church just after morning mass ended. The spectacular altar was still brightly lit. The wall of gold soared to a high, gothic arched ceiling. As we sat amazed, the lights switched off, leaving only the statue of the Virgin and Child lit in the low center, like a nightlight in the grey stone gloom.

Out into the Spanish sunlight and wandering downhill we found "Casa de Comida Begoña Antonio" and had our first *tapas*. We were joined by the French couple with whom we'd shared the taxi in Logroño. We all compared notes about where we all were staying. When we asked if they were staying at an albergue, she laughed and said she was doing the 'Camino of Hotels.'

Back at our albergue, beds were beginning to fill and a line had formed for the shower. Once again, I overheard someone meeting Dad, "You're Harold from Houston? I've heard about you!" It was a kick. An Australian who'd just been sharing with the general group his woes of tendinitis, looked up from his laptop and announced, "I've just posted 'There's an 82-

year-old gentleman from Texas walking the Camino, so I'll just stop my b——ing.'"

We took a quick nap then went out again, sat at the café and visited with our fellow peregrinos.

Elmarie (from Australia), the doctor who had phoned for emergency services to come for the woman who broke her leg on the path to the Alto del Perdón, was there. Now Elmarie took a long look at me and asked if I was well. When I confessed that I was not at full strength she questioned me. Hesitant to discuss the problem at the table, I asked her to stroll with me. As we stepped away from the rest of the group, I confessed the UTI, and she swiftly responded offering me a packet of antibiotic pills and writing a note for me to take to the local farmacia to get other (nonprescription) medications that would ease and accelerate my recovery. I came to realize over the course of the Camino, that many doctors were on the pilgrimage and many carried with them medications in case they or others needed them. This is the way of the Camino. The urge to help one another along the way—to watch for need and fill it where possible—is part of the pilgrim experience.

That night, in our luxury albergue, I was wakened repeatedly by the Spanish woman who was in the bunk at the foot of my bed. Apparently, my snoring was disturbing her sleep. Of course, we were in a room full of people snoring, but I was the one she could reach and on whom she was determined to take revenge by shaking my bunk to keep me awake. I became furious with her and finally flipped myself round so that my head (and snoring) would be even closer to her.

When morning arrived, the room began to stir and other pilgrims switched on the lights in the bathroom. As the door opened and closed the light fell across this woman and her companion who was sleeping in the upper bunk. She got up and turned off the lights in the bathroom, an exercise in futility as she and her husband were the only ones still in bed. Then the lights for the entire room came on. They were on an automatic switch set by the management. The twenty or so pilgrims packing up for the walk were glad for the illumination, but our bed-stuck amigos were having none of it. They kept reaching over and switching the light off even though it came back on after a few minutes.

I was still harboring a good deal of anger from having my sleep broken by the woman I had come to think of as "the Queen of Spain" and this game of on-again/off-again lighting was the last straw. I marched to the switch, flipped it to the on position and suggested in angry English that if they wanted to sleep late, they should get a room at a hotel. There was a brief intake of breath amongst the roomful of pilgrims, and then the rhythm of packing and shuffling began again. The Spanish royalty just stared at me.

## Linda's Journal

*September 16 –*
*I'm fending off a drippy nose and cough, as well as the other, and along with it all is the caffeine headache from no coffee. I am walking through Spain's wine country but unable to partake. I've decided to try and have a hot chocolate with breakfast if I can. That should cause no unnecessary pain.*

*I'm glad we'll try shorter distances. I'd like to be able to enjoy the walk rather than merely endure it. Though, when I calculate the distance we've traveled, I'm amazed to see 100 miles have been covered. Even with the shortened distances, we should have plenty of time to make our walk, even to Finisterre. So far, I must admit, there has been very little about this journey that felt 'magical'—okay, none of it has (that I can recall). Oh, wait, we were surprised by a marching band on the otherwise deserted way through Lorca, and we've seen almost every sunrise...still, the mystical experience has eluded me, and that makes me sad.*

*Today is the first day of our second week on Camino. Perhaps I'm asking too much of 'the experience' and myself? Perhaps looking for a mystical experience is exactly what prevents me from entering one? I have been focused on the bodily experience—the pain, thirst, hunger, fatigue. I have not been focused on work or home, and have no idea how it will feel to re-enter that world and rate-of-speed. Doing the blog is the closest thing to 'normal,' and it feels like it takes forever to do.*

## Harold's Journal

Day 11. September 16, 2012

Linda is still not completely well. We decided to take the bus to Logroño today and make the next three days be 10 km per day only. That will let us complete our walking by noon before it gets too hot. That will give Linda time to get well we hope. We ate breakfast in the Hotel Monaco. We walked down to the plaza late in the morning. Linda got a chocolate-filled croissant. We caught the bus for Logroño about 11:30. We took a taxi from the Logroño bus station to the hotel and arrived about 12:30. The room is air conditioned with a good bathroom. We rested and agreed to limit future days to 15 km or less.

The festival of San Mateo is in full swing in Logroño. Bands are marching in the pedestrian mall.
There are horse-drawn carriages with women all
dressed up, balloons, bubbles and children everywhere. We ate a Donor Kebab on Portales Street.
The kebab was excellent and inexpensive food. We
sat down and shared the table with a young couple
in the plaza. As we started introducing ourselves
they said, "Oh, you're the father and daughter on
the Camino." Seems that everyone knows us.

---

## Blog Entry — Tuesday, September 18, 2012

Rioja and Paella

Yesterday, we left Basque country (or was it the day before?) and entered the region called Rioja—wine country. It
is also paella country apparently. For the last two days, paella has been on offer for the pilgrims menu and we've
been loving it.

We had planned to walk 7 km today, from Navarette to
Ventosa and then go on to Nájera tomorrow. Plans on the
Camino, however, are ephemeral at best. We found ourselves on the road at 6:30 AM which put us in Ventosa at
8:30—far too early to stop for the day. So, we had some

*pan chocolate* (chocolate croissant) for breakfast and hit the trail towards Nájera (10 km further away).

Along the way, we passed a stone beehive-shaped building with an information sign telling the story of how the pilgrim, Roland (you know, Charlemagne's pal), killed the giant Ferragut who was (according to the informational signage) nine feet tall with "a nose span of length and strength of four men."

Wow. That must have been One. Strong. Nose.

In some versions of the tale, a stone from Roland's slingshot felled the mighty schnozz. The version we were offered today tells a different tale of a death thrust through the giant's navel.

While we were sitting and contemplating noses and navels, one of Dad's fans came by and asked if she could take our picture. We said yes, and after she took her photo, she offered to take one of Dad and me with my phone. I can't believe I haven't asked someone to do that sooner!

We arrived in Nájera just before noon and were met by other newly arrived pilgrims clutching their cell phones and telling a woeful tale. Today is a fiesta day in Nájera and, they told us, all rooms were taken in the whole town. The hotels were "complet." Dad and I decided to check with the *Oficina de Turismo* to see if they could find us anything and, if not, if they could book us someplace in the next town (and we'd take a bus).

There were signs indicating the way to the Turismo, but the way was far from clear. Happily, a lovely and kind teenaged Spanish girl chose to lead us there (rather than try to explain directions). The very nice lady at the Turismo made one quick call and we had a room with en suite bath only two minutes walk away.

We took baths and put on our last clean clothes. It was 1:30, time to go get lunch before everything closed for siesta. When we got to the lobby, we asked if there was a laundry service and, miracle of modern civilization, there WAS! Up in the *ascensor* (elevator) to stuff our laundry in a bag. Down again to hand it to our wonderful hostess and then out into a cool afternoon to find paella, grilled pork ribs (with the ubiquitous *papas fritas*—french fries) and flan (for me), ice cream (for Dad).

Back to the room we went for our own siesta, then out into Nájera for an hour of sightseeing. We visited the Monestario Santa Maria la Real (a lovely church and cloister built onto a cave in the hillside) and the Museo Najerillense (where artifacts from excavations near Nájera are on display including Roman and Neolithic pieces). We made our way back to the room to find our laundry done. Ahhhh.

Dad says we've gone 20% of the way. Only 370 miles to go!

# Notes

[1] Alvarez, Linda G. "Video of Parade." Web. http://youtu.be/guBzjAjHK08

# CHAPTER 10

# Nájera >
# Santo Domingo de la Calzada >
# Viloria de Rioja

R hythms of stride vary on the Camino, and pilgrims stop for rest at differing intervals. This means that over the course of a day or week, one is passing, being caught by, and repassing the same set of peregrinos. Usually this is a cheerful thing and happy greetings are exchanged, but now we were passing and repassing the King & Queen of Spain along the way. Every time I saw them, I relived my anger and the humiliation of having lost my temper. I wondered if I'd be walking with this sourness all the way to Santiago. The conflict we had in the albergue that night could not be left behind in the refugio. We were walking the same path and would encounter one another again and again. So as I walked, I began to think about how to restore congenial community. I thought about the Spanish woman's frustration with the lights and noise when she wanted to sleep. I remembered that I was carrying a sleep mask and several pairs of ear plugs to protect myself from those very irritants.

The weather had started to cool and we'd been walking under cloudy skies. We were glad for the cloud cover as most of the trails had been without shade and would have been very tough if the sun was out. From Nájera, we walked 15.1 km (about nine miles) to Cirueña. It was a fairly steep climb into Cirueña and the city fathers must have been *peregrinos* (pilgrims) because at the top of the hill, just at the city limit, they provide a resting place where weary pilgrims can put their feet up.

In the square, was a little gathering of tables and chairs. Across the street was a café. Skies were lowering with moisture-heavy clouds. Our plan for going only 15 km per day max meant that we needed to skip ahead from here to Santo Domingo de la Calzada by taxi. I went into the café and used the pay phone on the bar's counter to call for the taxi then went out to the square to join Dad. As I sat down next to him, the King & Queen of Spain arrived and settled at a nearby table.

Here in the square in Cirueña, with huge raindrops starting to fall, I dug into my pack, pulled out the sleep mask and
baggie of ear plugs and offered them to the Queen of Spain.
We didn't have a language in common, so this was all done
wordlessly. The act was enough to show that I had thought
about what the experience for her was like—and was offering
a way to ease her path. By doing it I also eased my own path
because later, when we passed one another on the Way we felt
a happy connection rather than the awkward friction (and, for
me, shame because I answered the conflict with anger and ag-
gression in my first response).

From Cirueña, Dad and I took a short taxi ride into Santo
Domingo de la Calzada. Once again, we arrived during a
citywide fiesta. This was the *Fiesta of Gracias* (Thanksgiving)
and St. Jeronimo Hermosilla.

Our taxi dropped us near the oficina de turismo where we
secured a room in the local hospederia run by Cistercian nuns.
As we made our way through the streets we ran into several
pilgrim friends who had arrived before us. The lovely and
kind Louise from Ireland led us through the crowded, winding
streets to our *hospedería* (guest house) where we checked in
and did the daily ritual chores (shower, hand wash clothes,
reshuffle pack contents). Out on the streets again, we worked
our way toward the restaurant recommended for lunch in our
guidebook. Marching bands, parades with dancing children
(playing castanets) and ambling dignitaries blocked streets
and, once we were seated near a second story window, sere-
naded our meal.[1]

After lunch we joined the rest of the city in siesta. We
woke again about 5 PM. At 6:30 we wandered into the church
adjoining the abbey to listen to the nuns sing vespers. Then

we were back outside wandering in search of dinner. We ran into Rick from San Mateo and Michael from Menlo Park who had been at the albergue in Orisson on our first night. They were thrilled to see Harold from Houston and the four of us found a nice little restaurant where we enjoyed *huevos con jamón y pimientos* (eggs with ham and peppers) and lively conversation.

Dad and I were back to our room with heads on pillows by 9:30. At 11:00 PM, the fireworks started. I sat up in bed, pulled back the curtain and watched the show from our window. Happily, it was not a long show and signaled the end of the outdoor partying. The streets below were quiet by 11:30 and I fell back to sleep easily.

---

## Harold's Journal

Day 14. September 19, 2012

Today makes two weeks since we left Houston. Linda's health seems to be improving but is not 100% yet. We walked 9 miles (15 km) today in 4½ hours that included a long breakfast stop in Azofra and a long rest stop. So, we made good time in spite of one hill in that span that rose almost 200 m in 5 km. It was a hard climb. We are in Santo Domingo de Calzada. We are staying in the Hospederia Cisterdense. We are in a very nice small room in the old city near the cathedral. The Festival of Gracias is in full swing. We had the pilgrim lunch at noon since the restaurant will be closed tonight. I am feeling great. We had a wonderful dinner with Rick and Michael. They both live near Linda in California.

## Linda's Journal

*September 19 –*
*Now we're back at the hotel—warm night—Dad is sleeping. I've had*
*a shower and am settling before sleep. The conversation tonight re-*
*minded me that my quest-ion is "What's next?" Where does the en-*
*ergy to DO flow?*

# Viloria de Rioja

The next morning we left Santo Domingo early and walked through a series of tiny villages crossing into the region of Spain called Castilla. Let me just say that the Castillians want to be sure you know when you enter their province. They provide a HUGE signpost trailside with a map showing the portion of the Way that lies in Castilla. As we passed through the villages, there were places set out just for weary pilgrims to rest and have a cup of water. In one, I stepped into the church (every village has a church) and was amazed at the opulence of the altar and the organ. We stopped at a café to visit with a few other pilgrim friends. Then, we planted our walking sticks to lift ourselves out of the chairs and followed the yellow brick road (literally, a yellow line had been painted on the stone street to guide pilgrims through town) on into Viloria de Rioja where we had made reservations for the night.

When we arrived at the albergue in Viloria del Rioja, we found two young women resting on its terrace. They were pilgrims from South Korea. Dad told them that he had been in Korea sixty years ago and they both smiled, nodded, bowed and said, "We respect you. Thank you." Then one of them went to her pack and came back with a small beaded charm which she set in front of Dad saying, "This is my gift to you. The symbol is Korean for happiness, good fortune, and wealth." I was struck by how deeply and personally these young women felt gratitude for my father's service, which took place decades before they were born. I could tell this was a completely new (and wonderful) experience for Dad. In the U.S., the Korean War is the forgotten war and he has rarely spoken of his time in the Navy.

Our new Korean friends asked why we were on the Camino, and we told our story again. Dad asked them why they were on Camino. One said she didn't know. The other said that she had many prayers for family and for a friend with cancer. She also said that she was unmarried and hoped some-day to find a husband and make a family of her own. Dad told her he hoped so too and that, as it happened, this very day was the day sixty-five years ago that he met his wife, and that next June would mark their 60th anniversary. I think we all took it as an auspicious sign.

The albergue finally opened its doors, and the proprietress announced that they were already full—all beds reserved. With much laughter and mutual picture taking we bade the two young women goodbye and they went on their way.

Viloria de Rioja is a cluster of ancient dwellings, neighbors and gardens, with no café or (so far as we could see) shop of any kind. In this hamlet, Orietta and her husband run a small albergue in their home, with no more than a dozen beds. Dad and I had arrived without any lunch, and Orietta told us there was no place in town to find provisions. In fact, the fruit truck had come through the day before and would not return until the next week. We were resigning ourselves to the squashed granola bars in our pockets when Orietta dashed upstairs to bring each of us a banana and small apple. Perfecto.

9-20-12 cont'd - the albergue in Viloria de Rioja is small, isolated, calm...very restful. There is nothing to do or see, so we have just rested & relaxed in the soft chairs - smelling our dinner cooking, waiting for socks to dry, wary eye on the gathering clouds. Two more days of walking then a bus to Burgos... there are some climbs & descents ahead of us... will we skip them all? I hope not.

The day was very hot and dry. Sitting in the shade outside the albergue I noticed that there were lots of vegetable gardens in the adjoining properties with tomatoes and peppers growing in abundance. I was reminded of Garrison Keillor's story about his Minnesota neighbors leaving bags of zucchini on one another's porches at night because of having too much produce from their own gardens. I thought about the high unemployment in Spain and the isolation of this and many of the tiny villages we had passed through on the Camino, and I realized that these backyard gardens were probably an essential community food source.

Orietta and her volunteer assistant (Ana from Brazil) cooked a huge dinner for the peregrinos sheltering together, and we sat around the table introducing ourselves and enjoying the bountiful meal. At the table were a Brazilian man traveling alone and happy to find another speaker of Portuguese, a 24-year-old German man traveling with his mother, and another German woman traveling alone. Dad and I were first to bed.

During the night I began to experience the first signs that all was not well with my digestive system. Knowing that we only had a short five-mile walk ahead of us, I took my time getting ready in the morning and by 8:30 was convinced that the trouble had—er—passed.

# Notes

[1] Alvarez, Linda G. "Video of Parade." Web.
http://youtu.be/cINRUDI_KWE

CHAPTER 11

# Viloria de Rioja > Belorado > Burgos

We had a very pleasant walk through a misty morning into Belorado, a bustling city compared to tiny Viloria de Rioja. We stopped along the way for a pastry at a café—it was cloyingly sweet. A little later, along the trail, Dad had to take a seat. He was feeling dizzy and sort of chilled. We put it down to the oversweet pastry. While we sat there, several pilgrims stopped to check that we were all right. One of them was my friend, the Queen of Spain. She stood on the path, looking at us and asking if we needed help. When we assured her we were just taking a quick rest and were fine, she nodded, said 'Buenos días,' (Good morning) and walked on. I was so relieved that the hostility between us was gone.

# Belorado

Having arrived in Belorado before our albergue was open, we sat at a café on the square, shaded by massive sycamore trees, and waited for noon. Our friend, Louise from Ireland, came through the square while we were waiting and exchanged a few words. Her time on the Camino (this trip) was coming to an end. Soon she'd be back in Ireland, planning to return another time to complete another section of the Camino. We were sorry to say goodbye. After Louise and her friends had left, a brief shower sent Dad and me scurrying for shelter under the stone arcade ringing the perimeter of the plaza. There we found a sign promising that we were only 534,4 km from Santiago (337.65 miles)—pilgrims' progress.

At noon, we checked into the albergue and were able to book a room in the adjoining *pension*—private bedrooms with shared bathroom down the hall. We took a quick nap and set out to see what sights we could find. As we passed the old church, we could see above us in the hillside, the caves where hermits used to dwell. The old hermitage caves have been updated and now there are windows and doors embedded in the hillside, a very novel sight. We looked into the church and marveled at the opulence (again) and took pictures of the two statues of St. James (St. Iago—patron of the Camino). One statue portrayed him as a pilgrim, the other commemorated his martyrdom by showing him holding his haloed (severed) head in his arms. We then strolled down to the oficina de turismo to see about a wifi connection (none at our albergue). We were given the password and told that the office was about to close for siesta. To actually use the wifi, we would need to return after they reopened at 5 PM.

We spent a leisurely afternoon in a café on the plaza. I wasn't feeling hungry and just had a small pastry with water. At the café, we visited with a couple from Washington, D.C. They were walking her second Camino and her husband's first. When the Turismo opened again, Dad and I went over. I text-chatted with Ric while Dad looked at the extensive exhibits. Then we sat on a bench just outside the door and Dad called Mom using the Skype connection on my phone. Amazing technology. I was feeling ready for another nap and Dad was, as always, accommodating—so back to our room we went. When dinner time rolled around, I found I still was not hungry and opted to stay in bed while Dad went off to dinner.

## Linda's Journal

*September 21 –*

*We only walked 5 miles today & it was a good thing 'cause I had diarrhea in the night (at VdR) and still feel less than 100% at 7 PM. Belorado is a nice little town. Has a great turismo office...but I've been uninterested really because I'm wondering when my body will at last decide to join the Camino in a positive role...first a UTI infection—and now a stomach/intestinal complication. WTF? It is like my body is fasting—or demanding a fast. No coffee or wine because of the UTI and now, limited food types...will I have the strength to walk 12 km w/ pack tomorrow? I guess I'll see.*

*Today is Ric's birthday. I Skype messaged with him briefly (ltd Internet). Dad has gone to dinner and I've stayed in the room because I feel full...the water I drank this afternoon seems to just be sitting in my stomach. I slept late this morning...took a nap at noon when we arrived here in Belorado and another at 5:30–7:00. I can't seem to muster the energy to go out—or even get out of bed. My heels hurt— the bottoms of them.*

*Dad says he's going to the 8 PM pilgrim's mass...I wonder if I will feel like going? Or if I'll stay in and have time alone...which I do crave.*

*Last night, in Viloria de Rioja, Orietta (the Hospitalera) said that one doesn't have to walk the whole 500 miles—or every step...for it to be a true Camino. I felt relieved to hear that from her. She recommended not rushing, but taking a bus to a place closer to Santiago and then walking from there. Of course, when I look at the 3D map of the last 100 km...it is mountainous. We'll be walking in mountains then...if we don't, we won't get the Compostela.*

*We started walking on the 9th. Today is the 21st = 13 days (the bell signaling the start of Pilgrim's Mass just rang) and we've done 10 of 33 'stages.' I don't know how many more stages to get to Muxia and Finisterre. 40 days and as many stages left to go...I believe.*

*I have one more antibiotic pill to take for the UTI and I'm afraid if I take it I'll barf it up...[sigh]*

---

## Harold's Journal

Day 16. September 21, 2012

Today is Ric's birthday. We had breakfast at the albergue and started walking at 8:30. We arrived at Belorado at 10:30. I had my first potato tortilla. It was good. We had a room in a pension reserved. It is a nice room. Linda and I both took a bath and a nap. We went to look at the ca-

thedral (an ancient fort converted into a
church). Behind the church in ancient times hermits lived in caves in the limestone hill. Some
of those caves have now been converted to apart-
ments. There are doors and windows set into the
limestone hill. The albergue has a pilgrim menu
at 7:00 and there is pilgrim's mass at 8:00. We
ran into Louise from Ireland again in Belorado's
main plaza. She took yesterday off and has less
than a week left on the Camino. There is an excellent tourist center here. It is a nice town
with a relaxed atmosphere. I had the pilgrim's
menu at the albergue. It was not very good. Linda
is not feeling well and she just stayed in bed
rather than eating.

---

By 3 AM I was full-on sick with stomach-intestinal distress.
I crawled back to bed and, in the morning, let Dad know that
we were going to need to spend another day in Belorado. As it
happened, I was not the only stricken pilgrim. The farmacia
was once again consulted. Imodium and electrolyte powder (to
mix into my water) were obtained, and I proceeded to sleep
away Saturday.

# Burgos

On Sunday, we took the bus to Burgos, the city where El
Cid was born and is buried. I was already on the mend but still
needing rest, so we checked into a hotel for two nights. I had
tea and dry toast for dinner and more of the same for breakfast, but I would need several days' break so I could regain my
strength before we set out again on foot.

Dad and I shifted into "tourist" mode, scoping out places
along the Camino with interesting sights and planning to

travel by bus and car until I was once again eating full meals and confident I could walk far enough to trek from town to town without assistance.

## Harold's Journal

Day 18. September 23, 2012

Linda is feeling better. She is sitting up, drinking water, and water with electrolytes. We plan to take the bus to Burgos at noon and stay there a couple of days to give Linda some time to recover. The people at the pension let us stay in the lounge and let Linda lie down on the couch in the lounge until time to leave and walk to the bus station. We arrived at Burgos at about 12:10. We took a taxi to our hotel that turned out to be a pension (no en suite bathrooms). We decided to not stay in the pension. I stayed with the *mochilas* (backpacks) while Linda walked down the street and found a hotel for us. The Hotel la Puebla—*uno hotel pequeño con carácter*—one small hotel with character. We booked for two nights.

## *Linda's Journal*

*September 23 –*

*I was not mistaken about the barfing. I've been ill with stomach/intestinal bug. Slept through Saturday—rode bus to Burgos Sunday—day of rest in Burgos. Monday and trying to plan the next few stages. What next town shall we choose to rest in? And after that? Where in the Meseta shall we skip to?*

## Blog Entry — September 25, 2012

To Meseta or Not To Meseta

Monday was a leisurely day in Burgos. We visited the cathedral and saw the spot where El Cid is buried (his wife is there too).

The cathedral is huge and thickly encrusted with decoration outside and in. The central sanctuary is surrounded by multiple small chapels constructed at various times, mainly (it appeared to me) as celebrations of—and ostentatious burial sites for—the respective Bishops who had them built. The artisanship was exquisite.

In places where worship has taken place for centuries, I almost always experience a strong sense of Divine Presence. The sensation was starkly absent in this cathedral. It was as if the Divine Mystery that greets us at the heart of beauty and in places of gathered worship had abandoned this one, leaving the beautiful objects empty, the structures serving more as testaments to human commerce and ambition than to the Mysterious Divine.

Perhaps it is my modern eyes that are blind to the symbols contained in the works that would evoke a deeper response had I better understanding.

The other order of business for Monday was to plan the next few stages of our trip. We have reached the eastern edge of the 'meseta'—over a hundred miles of landscape that bears a remarkable resemblance to Nebraska. My need for rest gives us an excellent reason to skip much of this section of the Camino, hopping ahead by bus or train. But where should we skip to? What next town should we choose to rest in? And after that, what next?

While I rested, Dad walked to the oficina de turismo to explore possibilities. Once he'd returned, we continued struggling to find some place along this stretch that would be worth spending a day or two. All we could find were more churches with ornate (and somewhat gory) altarpieces, or ruins high on hills overlooking otherwise sleepy-to-the-point-of-dormant villages. We were shaking our heads in frustration when Dad said, "Linda, I'm up for anything."

"Do you really mean that, Dad?"

"I really mean it. Anything at all."

"Want to go to Granada and visit The Alhambra?"

Matching gleams in our eyes, we headed to the Burgos oficina de turismo once again. The nice lady there recognized Dad with a big smile and in startled response to our request for help planning a jaunt to Granada, she said, "You do know that's a long way?" We assured her we had a map and understood the distances.

She found the train schedule, directed us to the train info and ticket office and by dinnertime we had train tickets for Tuesday and hotel reservations in Granada, as well as tickets to see the Alhambra on Wednesday afternoon. We are spending Tuesday traveling and will arrive in Granada about 10 PM. We will spend a day in Granada (maybe two—depends on room availability). Then we'll take trains and busses north and westerly to rejoin the Camino, hopefully at Astorga, where the guidebook says we will find a building designed by the famed Spanish architect, Gaudi.

Once back on the trail, the plan is to walk short distances for a few days to rebuild our strength. We will have replaced walking across the meseta with a train trip through Spain and a visit to a place I've always wanted to see and that Dad wished to but never believed he'd get to revisit.

# CHAPTER 12

# Granada

Our trip from Burgos to Granada was an all day affair. It began with a taxi ride to the Burgos train station where we discovered many other peregrinos gathering. Our train for Granada was scheduled to leave about an hour ahead of a train that was headed to Santiago. Most of the waiting pilgrims were skipping all or part of the Meseta and then restarting their walk further along the way. Our friend Francesca from Italy (who had occupied the bunk above mine in the Roncesvalles albergue) was there. She had developed tendinitis and, in order to complete the required final 100 km on foot within her remaining time, was taking the train to Sarria. A couple from Canada was planning to go as far as León and from there would recommence their trek. Johan from Holland was planning to take the train all the way to Santiago.

This was Johan's second Camino. He'd walked it once before from St. Jean to Finisterre, celebrating his ability to do so given that he has multiple sclerosis. This time, he'd experienced a flare-up of his symptoms in Burgos and so was now on his way to Santiago by train. As we were chatting, he received a message from his wife confirming his reservation at the Parador there (a luxury hotel located in a historic palace or monastery)—Dutch delight.[1]

We hopped on our train and settled in for the ride to Madrid, changed stations in Madrid (where we also half-guiltily ate Whoppers at the station's Burger King) and caught the next train that would deliver us to Granada just before 10 PM. An enthusiastic tour guide/taxi driver whisked us through the bustling streets of Granada pointing out the most important sights, "That restaurant has Very Good Tapas." When we arrived at our hotel, situated at the foot of the hill upon which La Alhambra sits, the desk clerk was standing on the sidewalk holding open the door for us and asking if she could help with our luggage. Two packs hardly counted as luggage, so we handled our own and she got down to the cheerful business of greeting us, orienting us to our neighborhood, giving us our room keys, and our tickets for—and tips on how to navigate—the next day's Alhambra visit. Exhausted and thrilled we made our way upstairs and fell into our beds.

## Harold's Journal

Day 20. September 25, 2012

Up about 7:15. Breakfast in the hotel. 52 °F and dry. Not as much wind as yesterday. Will check out of the hotel and go to the train station around 11:00. Linda had a first solid meal of roast chicken yesterday evening and is doing well this morning. Met Francesca (an Italian lady we met in Roncesvalles) in the train station. She just has 7 more days and was taking the train to Sarria. She will finish the Camino from there. Going toward Madrid the weather seems to be clearing. Arrived Madrid on time. Had a Double Whopper! and a Coke. Made the train station

change without incident. On the train to Granada
at 16:50. Arrives at 21:52. Oops! We stopped in
Cordoba at 19:05. Train reversed direction and
went backwards all the way to Granada. Arrived
Granada on time. Our hotel is great with a great
location part way up the hill to the Alhambra.

---

The next morning, with rain forecast for the whole day,
we headed out for what our map indicated would be a short
walking tour of the old city.

Maps are flat. Granada is not. It was a wonderful, winding
and tiring climb with so many opportunities to photograph
vistas and architectural gems that we progressed at a snail's
pace. Happily, we found a direct route down the hill for our
return to the hotel, where we took a (much needed by me) rest
before setting off up the hill to see the Alhambra.

Long lines and minimal signage greeted us at the gate but
we managed to find our way through the entry maze only to
discover that, once inside, there were even fewer helpful signs.
We returned to the gate and were told that there were no
maps of the complex available. We could clearly see other visitors holding maps but when we asked about those we learned
that those maps came only with the purchase of the audio
tour. Ah. So we spent our first hour and a half trying to find
the central palace and another forty-five minutes sheltering
from a downpour in the palace of Charles V.

Our tickets allowed us entry to the palace at 4:30 PM and
our delightful hotel receptionist had warned us not to be late,
"They are very strict. They will lock the gates." We were in
line in plenty of time with only sprinkles of rain falling. Slowly the line began to inch forward and then, we were in. The
crowds were so large, it was difficult to get a true sense of the

Alhambra's famous spaciousness and airiness, but the artistry and beauty were not wholly obscured and I began to worry that I might overload the data storage on my iPhone with all my picture taking.

Dad at La Alhambra. Note the growing beard.
He chose not to bring a razor on Camino

An hour and a half later, we emerged out into the gardens again and slowly made our way down hill, back to the arms of the most excellent Hotel Puertas de las Granadas. The long trip and extended walking seemed to set back my recovery, so

I spent the rest of the day mostly resting and reading, hoping to get digestion and strength back to normal soon. Dad was a champ, finding a restaurant to make white rice for me ("off menu" and for take out) and sitting patiently or napping while I rested and gathered strength.

Our plan was to head back north the next day, taking a train to Madrid and spend the night there. Then the following day, another train to Astorga where we planned to spend two nights before once again strapping on our packs and walking out toward Santiago.

## Harold's Journal

Day 21. September 26, 2012

Up at 7:00 and have worked through the map of Granada. We did a walking tour of the old city—excessive hills—too hard on Linda. Went back to the hotel for a rest and a nap before walking up the hill (about 20 minutes) to the Alhambra. Toured the Alhambra from about 2:00 till 5:30. Back to the hotel. Linda was exhausted and went to bed for some much needed rest.

Day 22. September 27, 2012

Linda still weak and not eating well. We have to change hotels today. Our present hotel will move the backpacks for us. We had croissants in the Plaza Nueve. Linda went back to the hotel to rest. I went to a travel agent to arrange travel and hotels from here to Astorga. We will take the train from Granada to Madrid tomorrow morning and overnight in Madrid. We have a hotel in the train station from which we will leave. We will go from Madrid to Astorga where we are booked into the Gaudi Astorga Hotel. It is raining again today. There is a protest against government belt tight-ening (austerity program) about 100 yards from our hotel. No one in the hotel or the streets seems to care except the protesters and the police. Foot traffic outside our hotel window is normal.

# Notes

[1] Van De Velde, Johan. "Essentis / Home." http://www.essentis.nl/ Web. 07 Oct. 2013.

# CHAPTER 13

# Astorga

The train trip from Granada to Madrid was more dramatic than we expected. On the day of our travel, Spain was experiencing torrential rains. It had been raining off and on in Granada but not enough to hint at the situation just a few miles west. We were standing in the train station waiting to board when the announcement came that there was a problem with the tracks between Granada and the next stop, so they were going to bus us all to the next stop and put us on the train there. We didn't understand what the problem could be until our bus was slowed to a crawl passing through high water and going around roads closed due to washout danger. We passed several drowning olive orchards. The bus delivered us safely and the train trip onward was uneventful.

## Harold's Journal

Day 23. September 28, 2012

Up at 6:00. At the train station by 7:45. Train
doesn't leave until 9:10. Tiny train station.
Nothing to do but wait. About 20 minutes until
our train was to arrive they announced that the
track was down and we would be bussed to another
train station. It turned out to be in another
town. The heavy rain had evidently washed out the
track. We finally got on a train at 11:55 at An-
taguera Santa Ana. Linda and I made a plan on the
train to stay in Astorga until October 4 and then
take 12 more days to walk to Santiago. Staying at
the Husa Chamartin Hotel at the train station. A
very nice hotel. Had another Double Whopper and a
Coke in the train station.

From Madrid, we took a commuter train (stops at *every*
stop) to Astorga where we checked into Hotel Gaudi, a lovely
place on the square with Gaudi's Palacio Episcopal and the
cathedral of St. Marta.

We'd arrived on a Sunday, so we spent it getting oriented
and making plans. Our plan was to stay in Astorga for four
days (leaving on Thursday). I was feeling much stronger and
starting to eat again. I had anticipated some weight loss on the
Camino, but nothing as drastic as what had resulted from my
illness. Now, I was glad I had chosen pants with drawstring
waistbands for my Camino clothing.

On Monday morning, to stay in shape, Dad strapped on his pack and walked to the next village where he had breakfast with other peregrinos on the Way before walking back. Tuesday was laundry day and Dad and I planned to do some more walking around the city. There were lots of sights to see in Astorga and the weather was absolutely gorgeous.

## Harold's Journal

Day 24. September 29, 2012

Up at 7:00. Linda okay but still on cracker only. 14 °C in Astorga. No rain for the next few days. Bought Elizabeth George *Believing the Lie*. On the train to Astorga at 11:40. I read about 100 pages of the Elizabeth George book—too many people with

too many problems I have little interest in. Arrived Astorga at 4:43. No taxis. Had to walk to
the Hotel Gaudí. We have a spectacular view from
our hotel window—the Bishop's Palace and the Cathedral St. Maria directly across the street.
Linda kept down yogurt and crackers.

## Linda's Journal

*September 29 –*

*We arrived in Astorga yesterday and plan to stay until the 4th, at
which point we hope to be back on the road, tapping our walking
sticks on cobbled stones at 7 AM and snailing up slopes to Santiago
and beyond.*

*I am watching people visiting Spain doing the tourist thing and am
feeling my own detachment from "sights." I just can't seem to connect
with the collection of "monuments seen" and, at the same time, am
not experiencing my trip as a connection or immersion in another
culture. I feel apart, and I wonder if "observer" is a habit of shelter?
Whatever this arms-length approach is—what does it serve? I don't
feel a nonverbal connection to Spain, the landscape, the culture, at
least, not yet. Granada and Astorga have been more comfortable—
certainly more so than the big cities, but there's no "tug," no mag-
netism in any of it, so far. Is it me? Am I demagnetized? I check
within myself for 'numb' and 'inert.' Those don't seem accurate. Still?
Yes, there is a stillness…like a rest note in a musical score; not inert,
a moment in between, a making of space—the space, when observed
with awareness, wants to fill with tears.*

*What the hell is going on? A month of illness has meant the total
unavailability of ALL my 'drugs' of choice—no coffee, no wine, no
food even, and no shopping. I've been able to read. My mind has not
wanted to take up any questions or board any trains of thought—*

*until today. Dad has gone out to sit in the square—giving me some space—and I'm looking inward, wanting to hear something, to know something—to feel something. It is like a fading of identity. I think I like it. No name...no face...no history or future...just daily life... toute sol.*

## Harold's Journal

Day 25. September 30, 2012

Up at 7:00. I walked to Murias de Rechivaldo (about 5.3 km). Had breakfast with other pilgrims and then walked back to the hotel. Linda had eaten yogurt and was doing okay. Linda and I went out to walk around town at about 11:00. Stopped for Linda to have tea in the hotel cafeteria. We walked a mile or so down the Camino and back to the hotel. We went out for a menu del dia. We both had a salad. Linda had beef and I had pork. Back in our room by 8:00.

Day 26. October 1, 2012

Up at 7:30. Linda had no trouble with the dinner last night. Looks like she has turned the corner. Linda and I walked to Murias, had breakfast, and returned to the hotel. I carried a backpack, she did not. We plan to make this same trip daily until she is ready to walk again.

## Blog Entry — October 5, 2012

Meson El Llar

We spent five nights in Astorga, resting, reading, eating. Every morning, Dad would get up, strap on his pack and walk five kilometers to the next town, Murias de Rechivaldo, where he would have a coffee and croissant, and then walk back to Astorga, just to stay in shape. I didn't go with him on the first day, and on the rest of the mornings, though I did go with him, I did not carry my pack.

In Murias we found one of the gems of the Camino, a small café called, Meson El Llar. The owner, Pilar, is an exuberant force providing handmade breads, cakes, and sandwiches including a vegetarian bocadilla made with organic produce freshly harvested from her garden.

On the morning I met her, Dad introduced me as his daughter. Pilar turned towards me with her arms open for an embrace and I found myself—under the spell of the tango music she constantly plays—slipping one arm around her waist, clasping her other hand in mine and spinning the two of us through the opening steps of a tango. A delightful meeting of minds and hearts and tango aficionados.

There is nothing to compare with a restaurant run by someone who lives to nurture others by feeding them beautiful food. All juice was hand squeezed to order. All dishes were prepared and presented with love and enthusiasm. Her artisan bun with fried huevo, jamón, and *queso* (cheese) made me pity the pale shadow of an excuse for food that is an Egg McMuffin.

## *Linda's Journal*

*October 2 – 3:30 PM*

*Dad is out in the hall on the phone with Mom (better signal out there). I texted with Ric earlier. Dad and I did a 10 km walk today (did one yesterday too). We walk from Astorga to Murias de Rechivaldo, have a coffee and toast, and then walk back. Dad carries his full pack (to keep in shape). I just carry water in my daypack.*

*On Thursday, we plan to have my pack ported ahead 10 km and we'll walk on, leaving Astorga at last and rejoining the peregrinos on the Camino.*

*This morning (Wednesday) I noticed that I was having the 'moment' that others had described back in Navarette...not wanting to do this Camino any more—finding it boring and pointless and wondering what was I thinking to even put myself here...and the moment passed.*

## Harold's Journal

Day 27. October 2, 2012

Linda and I walked out to Murias, had breakfast, and returned to the hotel. Linda had her first café con leche since the first day out of Ronce-valles. We plan to start walking the Camino again day after tomorrow. We are 164 miles from Santia-go. We visited the Palacio Gaudi. Very impres-sive. Gave me the sense of the Camino being something bigger than just a long walk. I feel more connected to the thousands of pilgrims who have made this pilgrimage in the past.

Day 28. October 3, 2012

Up about 7:30. We walked to Murias and had break-fast at El Llar. The woman who owns it promised a special breakfast tomorrow as we set out for San-tiago. Linda painted an old church with a stork's nest before we left Murias.

Back at the hotel we discovered we can send Lin-da's pack from here to the next place we plan to stop so she won't have to carry it.

Since my plan now was to have my pack ported rather than carrying it, I didn't want to leave the precious container of ashes in its secret pocket. I intended to carry Dustin's ashes with me as I walked, and wanted a small pouch that I could wear around my neck.

Dad and I searched the Wednesday market in Astorga to no avail. We were planning to leave on Thursday, and I knew I needed to find something before then, but we had not found anything suitable by dinner time. After dinner that last night, on our way back to the hotel, we passed a little store that had been closed every other day of our stay in Astorga. It was called "Merlin's" and now had kerchiefs, hats, and bags hanging outside its open doorway.

I stepped inside and asked the scruffy-bearded proprietor (who I thought must be Merlin himself) if he had anything like a little pouch that I could wear around my neck. He shook his head, no. My disappointment must have shown on my face because he immediately began rooting through the jumble on his shelves. With a shrug and questioning look, he held up a small rectangular red woven pouch with a bright green "Om" symbol embroidered on it. He was sorry that it was really meant to be a cell-phone carrying case and worried that it wasn't really what I wanted. To me, it was perfect. It hung from a braided cord designed to be a shoulder strap but narrow enough that I could wear it comfortably around my neck, and it had a flap with a Velcro fastener to keep the contents safe.

As I was paying for the pouch, Merlin brought out a small box with several open compartments. Several small stones and crystals nestled in each slot. He offered the box to me and Dad, telling us each to choose a stone to take with us on our journey. I chose a clear crystal about the size of a small cranberry. Dad chose a small colored pebble, and then Merlin insisted that Dad choose a second stone. The stones themselves seemed to represent for Merlin blessings that he wanted to send with us on our Way. We walked back to the hotel in the gathering twilight carrying the new pouch and our tiny blessing stones.

We did our nightly bag-packing and I carefully placed the little container of ashes in my pouch, along with the stone from Merlin, and laid it on top of the clothes I'd wear the next day.

Thursday morning, I left my pack in the hotel lobby with the "JacoTrans" envelope pinned to it. On the outside of the envelope was a form where I'd written my name and the name of the albergue where we had reserved beds for the night. Sealed inside the envelope was 7 Euro, the fee for the transporting service.

Crossing my fingers that the pack would indeed be with me again at the end of the day, I followed Dad out the door and we walked out of Astorga for the last time, finally on our way again to Santiago.

As we passed through, we stopped one last time in Murias to say goodbye to Pilar. She made a special "chocolate" for me—a cup of hot chocolate literally as thick as pudding. In it she mixed orange and cinnamon. Amazing. She toasted bread on the grill and served Dad's and my café con leche with the *tostada* plus fresh butter and honey so thick it spooned up and spread like jam.

While we were eating, a woman came out of the restroom holding a money belt and asking who it belonged to. Some poor peregrina had accidentally left it behind when she walked off. How dreadful to have to walk back from wherever she was once she discovered the mistake, but at least her passport and money were safe with Pilar.

As Dad and I embraced her and were saying our goodbyes, Pilar said to him that she had been born too late to know her grandfathers and that he would be her grandfather. Dad was happy to agree. We waved farewell and set out for the next small town, Santa Catalina de Somoza.

We arrived a little before noon to find my pack waiting for me against a wall of the café that served the albergue. We also found other pilgrims there with whom we had shared breakfast at El Llar. They told us that the lost money belt had been recovered. Pilar had been so concerned about the pilgrim-sans-documents that she had gotten in her car and driven along the Camino to try and find the owner of the money belt, and had succeeded in reuniting the two. This is how it is along The Way.

In the meantime, Dad continued to collect grandchildren. A pair of young men from Korea stopped for beer and rest in Santa Catalina and were chatting with Dad. When they learned he had been in Korea for the war, they spoke with deep gratitude of the sacrifices of American soldiers who died there and they thanked Dad and offered blessings and gifts to him for his service, calling him 'Grandfather' and asking to have their pictures taken with him. By latest count, he has collected a Spanish granddaughter and two Korean grandsons in addition to the Chinese granddaughter he picked up during law school (not to mention the seven grandkids and three great-grandchildren that came to him by the more conventional way).

There was no wifi service in Santa Catalina, so we had a lo-tech afternoon, lazing like lizards in the afternoon sun. From Santa Catalina we would walk to Rabanal. I planned to continue to have my pack ported for the next week or so while I got back in condition. I was beginning to think I might just have it ported even after I was back in shape. Walking free of the twenty pounds was a lovely feeling.

## Linda's Journal

*October 4 –*

*Staying @ El Caminante (albergue). It was a 10 km walk today and we arrived before noon. I felt ready for a break but confident that if it had been needed, I could have gone another 5 km this afternoon. My back is aching and I don't know if it is because of getting back to walking, or more ominous reasons (in the back of my mind I continue to monitor for symptoms re kidneys). I've bought a 1.5 liter bottle of water and am determined to drink it all today. Flush the system and focus on health. A pair of Korean young men stopped and chatted with Dad. Again he received gratitude and blessings from them when they learned he had been there for the War. They addressed him as 'Grandfather' and gave him gifts (in this case, Ko-*

*rean money). They spoke with gratitude of the American soldiers
who died in Korea.*

*Today we met Ingrid from Canada here—her feet are in bad shape
and Dad convinced her to stop walking for the day. She's a food
writer and is blogging for the Canadian Pilgrims organization.*

## Harold's Journal

Day 29. October 4, 2012

Up at 7:00. Checked out of the hotel about 8:15.
Linda sent her pack ahead to Santa Catalina where
we will stay tonight. Breakfast at El Llar in Murias (owned by Señorita Pilar). Srta wants me to
be a substitute grandfather since she never knew
her own grandfather. Arrived at Santa Catalina
about 11:00. Checked into Albergue Caminante.
Nice albergue. Linda doing well. Se Min Oh, a
young Korean man wants me to be his grandfather.
Lady named Ingrid is here. Janice and Bill here
as well.

# CHAPTER 14

# Santa Catalina > Rabanal del Camino > El Acebo > Ponferrada

W e spent Thursday night in Santa Catalina. Dinner was great fun because we were able to share it with a couple we had met on our first stop in Orisson and whose path we had crossed a few other times—Bill and Janice from Calgary. Together we celebrated that there was a wonderful cabbage and carrot soup on the menu. Things get pretty simple on the Camino. The next morning, we walked out of town early enough that the stars were still out, and I kept turning to look back and catch the sun rising.

## Rabanal del Camino

Our next stop was Rabanal del Camino. Our decision to walk shorter distances meant we were arriving at our daily destinations much earlier in the day. In Rabanal, the albergue we had chosen was on the eastern edge of town, run by a very cheerful and kind family.

We checked in, chose our bunks, and asked where we might do our laundry. Our hostess pointed to what looked like a small playground about a block west along the road and a few steps up from street-level. We could see some outdoor lounge chairs, what appeared to be a garden shed with a metal roof, and a clothesline stretched along one edge of the green space. This little park area, she told us, was for the exclusive use of albergue visitors. We gathered our dirty clothes and soap and towels in a bundle and climbed the little slope. Under the metal roof, we found a large sink where we hand-scrubbed everything, hung our clothes on the roadside clothesline and strolled back down the lane toward the albergue leaving our wet socks and underwear flapping in the noontime breeze.

Back at the albergue, we settled in at one of the outdoor tables to rest and watch other pilgrims passing by on their way through town. I pulled my watercolors and journal out of my pack and painted while listening to Dad and our hostess chat. After a bit, Dad and I moved to join some friends at a table outside the café to have some lunch. Lunch finished, I strolled back to the table where we'd been sitting earlier outside the albergue. I looked around for my little blue sack where I kept my watercolors and journal, but didn't see it. I had repacked them and left the sack sitting on the table (within view of my seat at the café) but it was no longer there.

I asked our hostess if she had seen it and she said, "Yes." She had seen another pilgrim pack it into his pack. Apparently, he had emptied his rucksack and repacked it at that table, accidentally taking the little blue sack containing my journal and watercolors and phone cord along with him. Our hostess remembered the little sack sitting amongst his things as he packed, but she couldn't recall what he was wearing, only that he was Portuguese. I could only hope that when he realized his mistake he would mail it all back to me at the home address I'd written on the cover of my journal.

Our hostess was less inclined to resign the sack to its fate. She dashed off to get her son who jumped in his car (with me in the passenger seat) and off we drove up the mountain track that is the Camino leading out of Rabanal. I kept wondering how we would find a person whose only known characteristics were his gender and nationality. My host/taxi-driver was not worried.

We drove all the way to the next village where he stopped in at every café and albergue to ask if they had a Portuguese pilgrim and to tell them our mission. Names and phone numbers were noted and promises given that they'd watch out for pilgrim and sack. Then, the son's phone rang. His mother had found our pilgrim back in Rabanal and recovered my sack. We backtracked to each albergue and café calling off the watch and then drove happily back to home base. This is the way of things on the Camino.

That evening Dad and I attended Vespers in the ancient church (along with our pilgrim pal from our first night in Orisson—Carol from Victoria). The priests and congregation sang vespers in Latin—a call and response Gregorian chant.

Afterwards, Dad, Carol and I went to dinner at the little café and the conversation turned, as it usually did, to what brought us each to the Camino and what we were finding there. I don't recall exactly what was said. We talked about what we hoped to learn as a result of our pilgrimage. I think we each held some form of the questions, "What next?" and "How can I live a life with real meaning and worthiness?" I do recall that, at the end of our conversation, I asked Carol if she would give me a blessing. I handed her my iPhone with John O'Donohue's, "To Come Home to Yourself" on the screen, and I knelt beside her chair. With her hand on my head she read it aloud:

> *May all that is unforgiven in you,*
> *Be released.*
>
> *May your fears yield*
> *Their deepest tranquilities.*
>
> *May all that is unlived in you,*
> *Blossom into a future,*
> *Graced with love.[1]*

## Cruz de Ferro

Up again with the dawn, we had café con leche with Marcel from Quebec and headed out for El Acebo. Everyone was looking forward to the day's walk with a mixture of anticipation and trepidation. Today we would pass the Cruz de Ferro (iron cross) where the tradition is for each pilgrim to leave a stone, symbolically representing the shedding of a personal or spiritual weight.

We also would be making a climb up and over a mountainside including a notoriously steep and rocky descent. Mindful of how difficult and dangerous had been the descent in the Pyrenees, Dad and I both had our packs ported and carried only day packs with weather gear and water.

We arrived at the Cruz de Ferro without difficulty. This is the place of the highest altitude along the Camino. The weather was cool but not cold, overcast but not raining. Perfect for the climb. We each took a moment to leave the stones we'd been carrying just for this purpose since we started.

Pilgrims on foot waited at the base of the tall pile of stones, allowing each other a solitary moment at the top.

Dad and I had finished and were standing at the base having our picture taken by a fellow peregrino when a group of bicycle pilgrims arrived. They sped in off the trail and without hesitation raced their bikes to the top of the stones—laughing and taunting one another, making a goal line out of what had been, until that moment, a contemplative, sacred spot.

I shook my head. It was my impression that bicyclists on the Camino saw the trail as a sporting event, an opportunity to conquer a variety of terrains at the fastest speeds possible. They rarely used bells and were often speeding up from behind and whizzing past startled pilgrims on foot. This disregard for fellow pilgrims was crystallized for me in the race to the top of the Cruz de Ferro. Even without what I thought was inexcusable rudeness, their speed and disregard for others were dangerous. We had already learned that a bicyclist had caused one walking pilgrim to fall and break his arm. Bicyclists have complained that they are not well treated on the Camino. Perhaps they might think about what sort of ambassadors for their sport they are being as they ride. Sharing with and caring for other pilgrims is apparently difficult to do while also racing for the 'win.'

Everything on the Camino is a metaphor.

As we left the Cruz de Ferro, the countryside once again became green and we enjoyed the mountain views as we walked. We passed through huge orchards of chestnut trees with their furry 'fruits' hanging on heavily laden branches. At one point, we were crossing a road. We were walking single file, as usual, with me in front and, as I was stepping out to cross, a truck began backing up to turn around. The way was steep and I wasn't sure what the driver intended to do—or if he had seen us—so I stopped. Dad smacked into me and then exclaimed angrily that I should have kept going. My choice to stop seemed foolish and dangerous to him.

I wearily thought I'd rather not be the one making the decisions for a while. I looked at him and said, "You lead for a while." He stepped out in front and started down the slope. In a very few minutes I realized that he must have been really holding himself back to stay at my pace all this time. Ten more minutes and he was so far ahead of me that I had to trot down the slope to try to keep him in sight. If I was going to have to run to keep up with my 82-year-old father, I was grateful we were on a downhill grade. If it had been uphill, I'd have been alone in a jiffy.

## El Acebo

The descent became steadily steeper and the path's surface was even more treacherous and long than we'd anticipated. The final kilometers into El Acebo were so steep that the dusty trail made multiple switchbacks. We had to be careful not to lose our footing on the dusty, gravelly path. As we approached the town, it seemed as if we could step off the trail directly onto the rooftops of the houses. It was with quaking knees and fulsome gratitude that we arrived at our *casa rural* (B&B) on the eastern edge of town.

In town we met a couple from New Zealand sitting at the café. She was having trouble with her feet because on the descents her toes were cramming forward against the front of her boots. It was a problem we knew others were having, and it created a great deal of pain for the walker. I was once again profoundly grateful for my own boots which I had thought were 'a half-size too large,' but now realized were exactly the right size for this long and difficult walk.

Many pilgrims were walking on to Ponferrada that day. I could not imagine going further and was content with our choice to save the last section of steep descent for when we were fresh the next morning. We performed the pilgrim's daily ritual: shower, laundry, eat, nap, eat, sleep, pack. We were up and away again by 8 AM.

## Ponferrada

The final leg of the descent into Ponferrada was just as rocky and steep as the day before, but not nearly as long. We arrived about noon-thirty, passing the huge Knights Templar castle at the edge of the 'old city,' then made our way to our hotel in the town's main plaza.

The hotel had a laundry service, so we collected our packs (freshly delivered by JacoTrans), showered and gathered every piece of clothing we weren't actually wearing to hand over for washing, drying and folding. Having your laundry done by someone else is the height of luxury. A good day of walking was appropriately celebrated with pizza and beer for lunch followed by an hour long nap.

We planned to cover another 15 km the next day. Since it would be fairly level terrain, Dad planned to carry his pack. I would continue to have mine ported at least until after we'd completed the last big climb up to O Cebriero (probably on Thursday). Looking at the maps and guidebook, we realized that we were probably about two weeks away from Santiago at this point. Amazing.

# Notes

[1] O'Donohue, John. "To Come Home To Yourself." *To Bless The Space Between Us: A Book of Blessings.* New York: Doubleday, 2008. 97. Print.

# CHAPTER 15

# Ponferrada > Villafranca del Bierzo > Vega de Valcarce > O Cebreiro

L eaving Ponferrada was a bit tricky. As the days grew shorter, we often would find ourselves walking out of town in the pre-dawn gloom. In the larger urban areas, the path is not well marked. Dad and I lost the way for a few blocks and were given remarkably bad advice on how to get back on track by two different people. Happily, we did not follow the misleading directions. Instead, we pulled out the incomplete map in our guidebook and made our best guess about which way to wander. To be strictly accurate, Dad led the way out of town based on his excellent sense of direction. If we had relied on my sense of direction, we'd still be wandering the streets of Ponferrada. We were back on the right path in fairly short order and soon were away from city streets and traffic.

Cloudy skies overhead kept us cool as the sun rose and provided a lovely rainbow on the hilltops as we turned onto a track that took us through the vineyards. It was harvest time. The leaves on the grape vines were turning. Families and communities were out in the vineyards picking the grapes together amidst shouted conversation and laughter.

## Villafranca del Bierzo

We arrived in Villafranca del Bierzo a good three hours before our albergue was set to open for the day. It was a drizzly day and the area where the albergue was located had only one café open. It was really a hotel and restaurant with a small coffee bar near the entrance and a couple of tables out on the sidewalk. The dining room was for overnight guests only, so we parked ourselves out on the sidewalk under the narrow eaves of the building, drank some café con leche and ate some cake while we waited for the rain to let up.

Later we wandered around town and found the supermercado where we met up with fellow pilgrims, including our friend Tina from Philadelphia. Together with their merry band, we hatched a plan to all get together later and cook a shared dinner in the albergue's common kitchen.

We checked into the albergue and discovered that the private room with two beds that we had reserved was a private room with bunk beds. I was going to have my first top bunk experience, enhanced by the fact that the narrow metal rungs on the ladder spun when I stepped on them. The need to call on my acrobatic skills was counterbalanced by the fact that the albergue offered a laundry service. Dad and I put on our rain pants and jackets and handed over every other stitch of clothing we had. Clean clothes are the basis of civilized society (that and hot showers).

We met our pals back at the supermercado at the appointed hour and were delighted to discover that one of the young men in the group was a chef. Did we like chicken scampi? You bet! We donated our Euros to the cause and stepped out of the way. Young people have so much energy at the end of the day.

Back at the albergue, our chef called us to the table to have guacamole as starters then chicken scampi with a lovely fresh salad. We also shared two bottles of local wine, one white and the other red. Both were lovely.

## Vega de Valcarce

Leaving Villafranca the next morning put us on an immediate, long and very steep climb. Relentless. As soon as we were certain we had passed over the peak, the path would take a turn and up we'd go again. Finally we were indeed on the way down just as sharply as we had ascended. By the time we reached relatively level terrain, we had spent four hours getting over the mountain. The remainder of the walk to Vega de Valcarce was a breeze by comparison. We were nevertheless very happy to sit down on the soft couch and chair provided by our B&B. There was no wifi in Vega de Valcarce. In order to make the reservation for the next night's beds, I had to ask our hostess if I could use her phone. As it turned out, she had a cell phone, and once she understood what we needed, she made the call for us. Kindness is part of the pilgrim experience.

We found a small grocery store about a block away from the B&B where we purchased a sandwich and the supplies for a spaghetti dinner. Our rooms were on the second floor of a small building that had a sitting room, dining room and kitchen on the ground floor. I cooked some spaghetti in the kitchen for our lunch, and we spent the afternoon napping and reading out on the upstairs balcony as a gentle rain began to fall.

## Linda's Journal

*October 10 –*

*We've had several days of steep inclines—both up and down—and rocky. We're nearly to Galicia and the weather has become decidedly Celtic—delightful when one is cozy in the casa rural watching and listening to afternoon rain—less delightful when tramping con poncho.*

*We walked from Villafranca del Bierzo to Vega de Valcarce today 'sin mochilas' (without packs) due to the steep climb and descent. Tomorrow we mount to O Cebreiro—another big climb (all day) and will have the packs ported again. The following day we hope to walk 20 km to Triacastela, and after that, I may once again carry my 20 lb pack...we'll see.*

*Today there is no wifi at our B&B, so we are doing without the call home...sad...the place is beautiful—quiet enough that I can hear the babbling water of the Valcarce river running through town. I've seen signs advertising fishing. The terracotta and dust landscapes have given way to green rolling hills, bird song and flower gardens under soft foggy skies, slate roofs rather than tile, white stone rather than brown/orange. The geraniums are just as red and lush as ever.*

*I am happy to have my feet up on my bed, elevated in hopes of avoiding swelling...middle age is an odd state for this female body of mine...*

## Harold's Journal

Day 35. October 10, 2012

Left Villafranca by 8:00. Terrible hill. Took 4 hours to go 10.7 km from Villafranca, just 1.5 hours to go the next 6.8 km. Arrived Vega de Valcarce at 1:30. Really nice casa rural. Saracen castle ruins high on the mountain overlooking the town. No rain but cloudy, cool weather. Rain forecast for tomorrow when we make the big climb to O Cebreiro. Started raining in the afternoon. Tomorrow, 10 km with a 700 m climb.

# O Cebreiro

When we woke the next morning it was raining in earnest. We pulled on our rain gear and checked the guidebook to confirm that today would be all uphill—15 km with a 2000 ft increase in altitude. We made frequent stops to rest, including a beautiful breakfast of farm fresh fried eggs and bacon in one of the little towns. In Spain, Coca-Cola is made with sugar rather than corn syrup and it was my 'drug of choice' today as energy for the ongoing climb.

At about the 13 km mark we crossed from Castilla into Galicia. The music in the cafés was now decidedly Celtic (bagpipes and tenors). As we arrived at the day's destination, O Cebreiro, it felt as if we'd hopped a continent and were in Ireland—rolling green hills being grazed by cattle with bells softly ringing in bone-chilling rain and fog. Our hotel was in an ancient grey stone building attached to the church.

Our packs had not yet arrived and so we waited in the crowded café—in our cold, soggy clothes—and watched pilgrims arriving while we remained ever vigilant for the JacoTrans van. When he did arrive, the driver put our packs in the lobby of the guesthouse where our rooms were located. We gratefully carried them up the steep, dark flight of stairs and got busy with hot showers and laundry. We cranked up the radiator heat and hung our socks along it under the windowsill. Once we'd changed into our dry clothes we went back out into the tiny hamlet of O Cebreiro where we spent the rainy afternoon and evening walking from shops to cafés and visiting with pilgrim friends. The town was packed with peregrinos and we gathered around fireplaces in the local bars, sharing stories and *vino tinto* (red wine). By the time we fell into bed, we had very little dry clothing left and even less hope that any of our damp things would dry out overnight.

Our guidebook forecasted a gentle downhill with minimal climbing for the next day, so Dad decided he'd carry his pack and we agreed to walk 20 km to Triacastela.

Closer, ever closer.

## Linda's Journal

*October 11 –*

*We walked in the rain all day—and uphill into Galicia. The weather has stayed rainy and is getting colder. It is very foggy up here. We are listening to Celtic music, experiencing Irish weather and landscape, and I'm loving it—feeling a bit of romance returning to the trip. Ric says they had rain and thunder in Half Moon Bay—first storm of the season. It will be holidays and winter when I get home.*

*I'm feeling tired and will be ready to sleep soon. Dad is already tucked in and dropping off. We will be walking 20 km tomorrow—only one short steep. The rest of the day should be level or downhill. Then, on Saturday, we plan to walk to Sarria. Sarria is when the final leg of the Camino begins. We will be about a week away from Santiago at that point. I'll take up my pack again—wow—suddenly, we are where the end is in sight. What an interesting feeling after slogging so far and thinking I'd quit.*

## Harold's Journal

Day 36. October 11, 2012

Left Vega de Valcarce at 8:20 in the rain. Rained all day. Mountain climb to O Cebreiro was difficult but not impossible. Both Linda and I ported our packs. Arrived O Cebreiro about 1:00. Made good time. Have a good place to stay.

# CHAPTER 16

# O Cebreiro > Triacastela > Sarria > Portomarín

It rained all night in O Cebreiro but morning greeted us with nothing harsher than a cold mist, so we fortified ourselves with café con leche and hit the trail. The guidebook promised we would start the day on "a delightful downhill path winding through enchanting woodlands." Reality proved to be a steep path climbing a further kilometer (or two) before descending for the remaining 12–14 kms into Triacastela. The good news was that though the descent was often steep and rocky, the rain had stopped so we were not contending with wet and slippery.

## Triacastela

Our B&B was on the westernmost edge of Triacastela. I couldn't decide if I preferred walking all the way through town at the end of the day (so that leaving in the morning would be simpler), or if I would rather stop at the first opportunity upon arrival at the day's destination. One feels differently about that depending on the time of day.

Happily, it was a small and level town. We checked in, took our showers, hand washed our clothes and hung them out on the balcony before going in search of our meal.

While it was not raining, the air was heavy with humidity and temps were quite chilly. We were not optimistic about the likelihood of dry clothes by morning. Two straight days of clammy polyester shirts—*ick*.

The café meal was much the same as they all had been— fried pork, fried potatoes and a plate of lettuce with tomato wedges with tuna as the 'salad.' I was less and less interested in eating. I didn't long for familiar food or home cooking. I just lost interest in meals, eating only enough to quell hunger and thirst, then leaving the remainder untouched.

We didn't see familiar pilgrim faces in Triacastela, so we made an early night of it.

## Harold's Journal

Day 37. October 12, 2012

Columbus Day. Holiday. Left O Cebreiro at 8:30. Walked 14 hard miles with a full pack. Worn out when we arrived in Triacastela at about 3:00. Linda ported her pack but plans to carry it to-morrow. We plan to walk about 12 miles to Sarria.

Day 38. October 13, 2012

Walking at 8:30. Rain and low 50's. Rained all the way to Sarria. Had a good breakfast of eggs, orange juice, toast and café con leche. Good lunch—spaghetti with meat sauce. Arrived Sarria about 2:00.

# Sarria

We woke to more mist and chill, dressed in our still damp clothes, and lashed soggy socks to our packs (hoping that there would be sun to dry them on our backs as we walked) but it continued to drizzle, so we tossed our ponchos over the top of the whole shebang and squelched our way out of town. This day's destination was Sarria.

At Sarria we would be just over 100 km from Santiago. To get the Compostela (certificate for completing the Camino) one must walk the last 100 km. Upon arriving in Sarria, taxis, buses, trains, bicycles and even horses would no longer be an option.

Sarria is the outermost town of any size on the Camino that is more than 100 km from Santiago. Consequently, it has long been a traditional starting place for pilgrims who wish to walk only the final 100 km required to obtain a Compostela.

We soon discovered that our pilgrim path had been joined by tour groups of peregrinos, fresh to the trail, chattering and stopping often to photograph one another by trees, way-markers, fields, and stone walls. We veteran pilgrims just shook our heads, exchanged knowing glances, and kept walking to a steady rhythm.

I was carrying my pack again, having been pack-free since leaving Astorga, and this day would test whether I was back to full strength. While it was a long walk, I found I was able to keep up the pace, and we arrived in Sarria weary but in plenty of time to find shops still open and to purchase the bits and pieces we needed to replace dwindling supplies.

As we were climbing towards our albergue—literally climbing several flights of stone steps—a pilgrim woman we had never seen before came running up to Dad and asked, "Are you from Texas?" When he replied in the affirmative, she said, "I've heard about you! A Canadian lady showed me your photo and told me about you." Yes, his fame was spreading up and down the Camino. Now that there were photos, there were also 'celebrity sightings' of Harold from Houston.

This delightful lady and her husband were from Scotland. They could see that we were just arriving and were feeling daunted by the long stretch of stairway that lay between us and our bunks.

She offered encouragement about the stairs, "You're nearly there!"

Dad joked, "Will you carry me?"

She replied with solemn sincerity, "I will carry your pack."

It was a breathtaking and devastating offer of kindness. I hoped he would accept and allow her to do this for him. I knew his feet were hurting because we had stopped at a pharmacy at the base of the hill to purchase pads for the balls of his feet. He declined the offer, determined to power up that hill on his own steam. So we parted from them with gratitude for their caring and set off to conquer the stairs.

We had a good rest that night at the albergue where they offered laundry service—oh the rhapsodies that I could sing about clean, dry clothes! We left Sarria about 8:35 AM and by noon had passed the marker indicating the point at which Santiago was only another 100 km away. A truly important (and literal) milestone of the journey.

# Portomarín

Coming into Portomarín, we crossed a long and dizzyingly high bridge over the river Mino, only to find at the end a tall set of stone steps leading up to town. Dad marched up them without hesitation. I took a picture as he started the climb and then followed him up.

The view was spectacular. The rain had stopped. We were dry and now within 90 km of Santiago.

Our hotel was on the outside edge of town and it took asking directions from a local before we could find it. After wandering through the main square and several side streets, we finally arrived and checked in.

Our room was only one floor up, so we carried our bags up the stairs rather than waiting for the elevator. Down a long hallway we found our door but couldn't unlock it with the key-card provided.

Back down the stairs again to get the receptionist to come and show us the precise combination of wrist-twist and card-jiggle required for admission to the charming suite. There was a sitting room, a full bath, and a bedroom, all decorated in Eisenhower vintage.

We rinsed out a few things and then settled in the sitting room to check our maps. If knees and weather held, and if all else went as expected, we would walk into Santiago on Friday!

As the dinner hour approached, we went back downstairs. In the lobby we found stacks of roly-cart luggage belonging to a prepackaged Pilgrimage Tour Group—one of two such groups staying at this hotel—each with a staff to accompany them and arrange their meals, lodging and luggage transport.

In the dining room two long tables were laid out for the tour groups, and a small corner table was set for Dad and me. We ordered our meal and, as we waited, the Prepackaged Pilgrims began to arrive all dressed neatly in nice dinner clothes.

Feeling grubby in my road-weary hiking gear, I pondered the joys of having someone to carry a suitcase full of multiple outfits—choices beyond two pairs of rip-stop pants, two quick-dry T-shirts, and dorm-appropriate pajamas. Some pilgrims have a more ascetic experience than others.

---

## Harold's Journal

Day 39. October 14, 2012

Walking at 8:30. Continental breakfast. Good lunch—2 fried eggs, cheese and bread. Walked about 22 km. Our longest day so far. No trouble. Arrived in Portomarín about 3:30.

Day 40. October 15, 2012

Good breakfast at the hotel. We are now overrun with plastic pilgrims. Two large groups. Temperature in the high 40's. Dry but heavy mist. No rain all day. Last serious climb on the Camino. Arrived Eirexe at 1:30. Included a long mid-morning break for café con leche and rest. Jim and Michelle at the same albergue as we are.

CHAPTER 17

# 5-4-3-2- . . .

## Eirexe

From Portomarín, we walked to a tiny place called Eirexe. Rain fell all day—a steady drizzle with occasional drenching showers. Under my poncho, windbreaker, and long-sleeved T-shirt, I found myself sweating in spite of the chilly temperatures. The gear was keeping the rain off, but I still felt soggy to the skin.

My drippy nose had turned into a sore throat and cough. At the little café across from our B&B, I ordered a whiskey, a lemon wedge, and a cup of hot water, and made myself a 'hot toddy.' Dad and I ordered a meal and then lingered through the afternoon, sharing our table with friends who arrived later and would be staying at the same B&B and greeting other pilgrim friends who were passing through on their way to stops further along the path. I was grateful to be out of the rain for the day.

# O Coto

The next morning we got up and walked another day in the rain, this time stopping in O Coto. O Coto is so small that the only thing there is the B&B where we stayed. The proprietress was a raspy-voiced, belly-laughing soul who asked how old Dad was. When I told her she exclaimed, "Ay, que guapo!" Yes, he does look great. She fed me chicken soup (for my sniffles) and fed Dad a thin beef steak and fries, all the while patting one or the other of us on the arm and bellowing out some jovial comment we could not understand.

In the lobby a bobbin lace project-in-progress sat on a table in the corner. The ladies in this part of Spain are famous for creating fine handmade lace, and it seemed someone in this little casa rural was carrying on the tradition.

In wakeful moments during the night, I listened to the rain coming down in sheets. My socks were hung on the heater in hopes they would be dry by morning. Looking at them, I suddenly realized the practical logic of stockings hung by the chimney with care—it's not just about Christmas presents. I felt foolish for never having made that connection before.

The rain was still falling heavily as we ate our toast and drank our café con leche in the morning. Our hosts shook their heads and waved their arms, fingers fluttering to demonstrate just how much rain was falling as they shouted, "*Lluvia!*" (Rain). Yeah, we knew. Rain. Lots of rain. We pulled on waterproof rain pants, ponchos and hats and set out. It rained all day again. We walked up hill and down dale along muddy woodland paths. Beautiful, lushly green, soggy landscape.

Dad and I stopped about midday at a tiny café. It was crowded with pilgrims sheltering from the rain under a blue tarp stretched over outdoor tables and chairs. We greeted pilgrim friends as we sat down and turned our attention to our Cokes and potato chips (the best sustenance on offer in that café).

The couple at the table next to ours did not appear to be pilgrims. They weren't wearing the 'uniform' of hiking boots and rain gear. The gentleman greeted us and asked about our Camino, where we started, when, and (of course) about Dad's age and health. He then told us that he was a taxi driver from Santiago and the young woman with him was his niece. He was driving her to Sarria so that she could start her pilgrimage there. We all commiserated about the rain and the walking, then he and his niece stood up to go. We said goodbye and joked with him, "See you in Santiago!"

## Arzúa

By the time we finally reached Arzúa, the day's destination, we were soaked through. We stuffed our boots with newspaper so they would be dry in the morning. Our clothes we draped over the heaters so we could pack or wear them the next day when we walked to Arca O Pino, about 20 km. The day after, if our plans held, we'd arrive in Santiago. The weather forecast taunted us with pictures of suns overlaid with raindrops. What did that mean? Hopefully, it meant—rainbows.

## Linda's Journal

*October 16 –*

*For weeks now, Santiago has been 500 miles away and now, suddenly, it is only 3 days' walk! We expect to arrive there on Friday the 19th. I've made reservations for two nights at the deluxe Parador Hotel there (haven't told Dad—just said that I picked a hotel with enough stars that they should have a laundry service. He's delighted by that). Given the time we have remaining, we've agreed to take a bus to Muxia and Finisterre rather than walk, and then see if we can get to London early and spend a few days there.*

*Tonight at dinner, Dad talked about the things in his life that have turned out to be the most important to him—and it comes down to being part of a chain of creating better lives through example, relationship, and mentoring. The resumé achievements, he said, seem hollow to him—but knowing that his life and example have encouraged others to live happier, fuller, more meaningful lives and to have been the recipient and re-transmitter of great mentorship is what glows for him as he looks back over eighty-two years. So that's an answer to one question I hoped this Camino with Dad might answer.*

*We don't all win the big prize, or have fortune or fame, or invent great cures, but every one of us can be part of a chain that creates ever-increasing happiness for all beings, and that is what makes a meaningful life.*

## Harold's Journal

Day 41. October 16, 2012

Started walking in rain at about 8:20. Temperature in the high 40's. Rained all day. Walked 17.18 km. Arrived at Coto about 1:30. Plan approx 20 km each of the next 3 days. Expect to arrive Santiago Friday.

Day 42. October 17, 2012

Started walking in the rain at 8:45. Arrive Arzúa at 2:15. Decided to not walk to Muxia and Finisterre. We'll just take the bus to visit those places. Trying to change airline reservations to leave October 24 if possible.

---

In Arzúa, we spent the afternoon phoning (via iPhone Skype) our various airlines to change tickets. We couldn't arrange any layover days in London, so we decided to just go on home. We'd be getting home a week earlier than expected!

---

# Arca O Pino

The walk to Arca O Pino was damp but not as miserably rainy as the day before. We found our B&B, did our hand-laundry, had our showers, and wandered back the way we'd come to see what we could find in the way of an evening meal. We found a place that styled itself as a 50's rock n' roll diner. Dad gave their hamburger a try. In Spain, 'hamburgers' are made with ground sausage rather than ground beef. I opted for the roasted chicken Pilgrim's menu.

While we were eating, Catherine from the U.K. came in. She and her companion joined us at our table. Catherine had been Dad's buddy in Belorado because her Camino partner, like me, had come down with the Pilgrims' Plague there.

Catherine and Dad reminisced about how much they'd enjoyed the conversation back in Belorado during their evening meal (the one I'd slept through). The pilgrims gathered around the table that night had shared thoughts on what insights they were experiencing on Camino. Many pilgrims along the way had asked Dad for his insights or lessons learned from walking the Camino. That night in Belorado, he told his fellow pilgrims that he hadn't really found new insights to share that are specific to the Camino, but he did have 4 principles that continued to hold true for him:

1. Abandon your life to God
2. Give up selfish desires
3. Let go of results
4. Let go of expectations

Now, in Arca O Pino, Catherine was delighted to reconnect with Dad and asked him to tell her again the four principles so that she could write them down. She wanted to remember them. Then Catherine showed us the Pilgrim's prayer that had been handed out at one of the stops along the Way.

## PILGRIM'S PRAYER

Although i may have traveled all the roads,
crossed mountains and valleys from East to West,
if i have not discovered the freedom to be my self,
i have arived nowhere.

Although i may have shared all of my possessions
with people of other languages and cultures;
made friends with Pilgrims of a thousand paths,
or shared albergue with saints and princes,
if i am not capable of forgiving my neighbor tomorrow,
i have arrived nowhere.

Although i may have carried my pack from beginning to end
and waited for every Pilgrim in need of encouragement,
or given my bed to one who arrived later than i,
given my bottle of water in exchange for nothing;
if upon returning to my home and work,
i am not able to create brotherhood
or to make happiness, peace and unity,
i have arrived nowhere.

Although i may have had food and water each day,
and enjoyed a roof and shower every night;
or may have had my injuries well attended,
if i have not discovered in all that the love of God,
i have arrived nowhere.

Although i may have seen all the monuments
and comtemplated the best sunsets;
although i may have learned a greeting in every language
or tasted the clean water from every fountain;
if i have not discovered who is the author
of so much free beauty and so much peace,
i have arrived nowhere.

If from today i do not continue walking on your path,
searching and living according to what i have learned;
in from today i do not see in every person, friend or foe
a companion on the Camino;
if from today i cannot recognize God,
the God of Jesus of Nazareth
as the one God of my life,
i have arrived nowhere.

Fraydino

# Harold's Journal

Day 43. October 18, 2012

Changed my plane return to 10/24/12. Dry this
morning. Praise God. Hope it stays dry. Forecast
looks hopeful. Didn't rain. High 50's. Arrive Arca 2:00. Dinner at a local bar with several pilgrim friends.

# CHAPTER 18

# Arrival

We left Arca O Pino at 8 AM. It was still dark as we walked out of town to the point where the Camino left paved roads and turned off into a dark wood. Really dark. As we stepped forward into it, we were immediately presented with a fork in the path and no arrow or marker visible to indicate which way we should take.

Three other pilgrims joined us. A couple of us had tiny lights (a headlamp and a keychain flashlight) and we cast the beams about in search of a marker. All we could see were the light-beams' glowing reflections against the dense morning mist. One of the others returned to the point where the dirt path met the pavement and came back to report that someone had drawn a supplemental arrow on the signpost which seemed to indicate the left-hand path. So we struck out in that direction. Another metaphor—stepping onto the dark path, choosing the way on the strength of faith.

As we walked through the mist, I contemplated Dad's four principles. 'Let go of results' was uppermost in my mind because as the morning wore on it became evident that the symptoms of my UTI were returning, possibly jeopardizing my ability to walk the final 17 km of the Camino. Catherine had spoken about a book she'd read called *Walk in a Relaxed Manner* about lessons of the Camino (by J. Rupp). I tried to walk in a relaxed manner so that I wouldn't make my symptoms worse by adding anxiety.

I thought about the way our minds dealt with walking every day—not focusing on the distance overall, just the distance today, the place to sleep and eat and wash—and how suddenly the last days of the walk seemed to appear. For weeks, I'd been thinking about walking 500 miles and now it was just a few kilometers. I thought about BIG projects waiting in my future, and about keeping focused on one part of the plan at a time, then persevering until suddenly the finish line would appear.

I also thought about intuition and how often we had stopped only two or three steps along a turning because it 'felt' wrong, then gone back to discover that we had indeed missed a way marker, an innate knowing that was not based on familiarity with the route or landscape—just a sense that we had left the true path.

EVERYTHING on the Camino is a metaphor—dammit.

Eventually, we emerged from the dark and misty eucalyptus forest onto a road with a Camino marker. Rejuvenated and reassured, we walked briskly on as the sun rose in a clear sky and cool morning. Hurray! No rain in the forecast. We would be walking into Santiago in the sunshine.

There was an eagerness and optimism to our walking. We had walked longer distances the two preceding days so that the walk into Santiago would not be a strain. We climbed what we knew was the last hill and stood at the top looking for landmarks the guidebook said we'd find there. Mist in the valley obscured the view, so we didn't see the spires of the cathedral from our hilltop. We somehow also missed seeing the famous statue of pilgrims overlooking Santiago, which is on that hilltop somewhere. Apparently one must turn off the path to find it, and we missed the signs that might have directed us.

I have to admit that I didn't really mind missing a side trip at that point. I was pretty focused on getting to the Cathedral and (figuratively) setting down the backpack for the last time. I could feel the discomfort of the UTI symptoms increasing. Eyes forward, stride lengthening, I kept walking, determined to finish under my own power—and finish we did.

## Santiago de Compostela

Downhill and down stone steps, we came to the edge of the city and plunged into a world of crosswalks, roundabouts, traffic and noise. Constantly scanning for signs pointing the way, we steadily walked our way deeper into the city.

The policemen's union was demonstrating, and for a while we were caught in the midst of a slow-moving crowd of uniformed men. We finally broke away and crossed the street. We had not seen any other pilgrims since entering the city, and were beginning to worry that we had lost our way. We had no choice but to follow the path of scallop shells embedded like brass breadcrumbs in the sidewalk. At last we spotted two tall, confident-looking, Nordic pilgrims marching a few paces ahead. If we were on the wrong track, at least we had company.

Very soon we could see that we were indeed on the right track as the spires of the cathedral came into view between the buildings ahead. Alert to the subtle shifts in direction indicated by how each shell was oriented in the pavement, we worked our way through the ever-older streets. We heard a bagpiper in the distance, and then passed him as we descended into the square...and arrived.

There it was—the cathedral and the square full of pilgrims just leaving the noontime mass. We hugged each other and as we stepped forward heard a shout to our left. The pilgrim couple from New Zealand, whom we had met in El Acebo, was right there to greet us with hearty and joyful congratulations. Pictures were taken. Tears were shed (by me). Hugs all around.

They gave us advice about when to arrive to be sure we were able to get a seat at the next day's Pilgrims mass (be there about 10:30 for the noon mass) and they gave us directions on how to find the Pilgrim Office where we could get our Compostelas.

I asked Dad if he wanted to go straight to the office for the Compostelas or if he wanted to check in at our hotel first. He suggested that we go to the hotel and get their stamp first, then go to the pilgrim office. I had made the arrangements for our hotel, so it was up to me to lead the way. I turned and headed across the square, pointing to the large, historic building along one side of the plaza. "That's our hotel."

"You did great," he said, "That's easy to find...oh my...it's the Parador."

"My treat."

We checked in to our luxury accommodations, dropped our daypacks and headed back out in search of the pilgrim office. We found it with little trouble and joined the long line of pilgrims. We had arrived at the cathedral at 1 PM. By 2 PM we had our Compostelas.

On our way back to the hotel, Dad dodged into a souvenir shop to buy two carrying tubes to put our certificates in (so they wouldn't get damaged on the way home) and ran into Rick and Michael (from California), the friends with whom we'd shared that first pilgrim dinner at Orisson and another wonderful meal and conversation in Santo Domingo.

We all embraced and celebrated reuniting here in Santiago. We exchanged contact info and then Dad and I started across the square again. Halfway across we ran into Lena (from Denmark), another fellow pilgrim. Hugs and joy and congratulations, and finally we were back at the Parador. By 3 PM

I had arranged to see the hotel doctor, and we had delivered our clothes to the hotel laundry and received assurances that we would have clean clothes by 8 PM. Bliss.

## Harold's Journal

Day 44. October 19, 2012

This is the day to walk into Santiago. Walking at 8:00. Dark with heavy mist. Cleared early. Sunshine and no rain. Passed Santiago city limits sign at 12:00 noon. Arrived at the cathedral at 12:45. Linda gave me/us 2 nights in the Parador Hotel. We checked in and went for our Compostelas. Ran into several pilgrims we met on the Camino—Mike and Rick among them. Carol is here somewhere. Hope we find her.

## Linda's Journal

*October 20 – 5:30 AM*

*Awake—thinking about the Camino. It provides a break from 'normal' life—and fills a human need (?)—for purpose/meaning by setting a task, a focus—single pointed. I feel as if the weeks have passed very quickly, without noticing. Now when I turn back towards normal, I see the difference—a difference—and I wonder whether my life will still fit me when I return to it. My clothes will fit differently (for a while at least). Will I go back to how I was? Or will the changes be permanent?*

*I don't feel like I've walked 500 miles…400? (we did skip the Meseta). I feel like I've walked 6–10 miles a day. I have a stack of days, fad-*

*ing images, blurring...not a single, mammoth ACCOMPLISH-MENT.*

---

Breakfast at the Parador was AMAZING. A huge buffet of fruit, yogurt, pastries, cereals, eggs, bacon, quiches, coffees, teas, juices, white linen tablecloths, silver coffee pots on the tables, uniformed waiters and hushed conversation. What a contrast to the crust of bread and scrape of jelly every other Pilgrim breakfast had been. I kept wishing I was hungrier, so I could eat more of the wonderful food.

After breakfast, we set out into the clear, crisp morning. It is great fun to be in the square when a pilgrim arrives. Almost always they will walk into the square to be greeted with a shout by fellow pilgrims whom they have come to know on the Way and who have arrived just ahead of them. The joy of the celebrations is sweet and deep, a sort of ecstatic agony of weariness blended with triumph. Some fall to their knees. Others lie on their backs with arms flung out, looking up at the spires of the cathedral against the bright blue sky.

While we were there, a young family we had seen in Rabanal—father, mother, two young children and a dog—arrived. They walked to the far edge of the square away from the cathedral and sat down on the stone pavement, hugging the children and waving off tourists who were trying to take pictures of them.

Dad and I walked slowly around the cathedral, then up the tall staircase and into the sanctuary.

## Linda's Journal

*October 20 – 10 AM*
*We are attending the 9:30 service sung and chanted here in Santiago*
*Cathedral with Eucharist. This morning, we visited the relic of St.*
*James, embraced the golden statue (from behind) during the start of*
*the service and then came to sit here on a pew to the side to listen to*
*echoing prayers and songs—male voices, Spanish language, soft foot-*
*steps of other visitors wandering through the cathedral. Call and*
*response in song—all congregants, male and female voices—nuns*
*wearing habits—huge organ, bells ringing overhead—smell of clove*
*incense.*

## Harold's Journal

Day 45. October 20, 2012

Up at 7:00. Breakfast in the Parador Hotel. A
wonderful room and a wonderful breakfast at about
9:00. Linda and I went to the cathedral. Saw the
relics. The handprint in the column is protected
with a steel banister so we couldn't put our
hands in the print. Embraced Santiago from behind. Went to early mass. Got a front seat on the
side. Spent a lazy day watching and greeting pilgrims as they arrived.

The day we were there, the ceremony with the *botafumeiro*
(a massive, incense burner that is swung from the ceiling over
the heads of the congregation[1]) did not happen. That spectacle
is only performed on feast days or when someone pays the
Cathedral a fee of 300 Euro. People do sometimes pay for the
ceremony as a remembrance in honor of persons or events.

We heard that they swung the incense the day before we arrived, and were going to swing it on the morrow, but Dad and I had other plans for the following day.

# Notes

[1] "Incense Burner at Cathedral - Santiago De Compostela." *YouTube.*
YouTube, 16 June 2012. Web. 07 Oct. 2013.
http://www.youtube.com/watch?v=oFd8JVYks5M

# CHAPTER 19

# The End of the Earth

After we had obtained our Compostelas, handed in our clothes for washing, and were standing at the concierge desk asking about the bus to Finis- terre, Dad and I each felt a tap on our shoulder. "*Hola, amigos!*" It was our friend the taxi driver from the blue-tarped café on that rainy day between O Coto and Arzúa.

We were as delighted to see him as he seemed to see us, and the concierge said (pointing to our friend),"He is the best taxi driver in all of Santiago! You should have him drive you to Finisterre and Muxia." So that is what we did. We arranged with José that he would pick us up at ten on Sunday morning and take us on a day trip, a scenic drive winding along the coast up to Finisterre, then to Muxia, and back to Santiago. Then José offered to drive us for free to the travel agency where we could complete our travel and lodging arrange- ments for heading home.

The drive on Sunday was amazing. José pointed out and explained the importance of '*hórreos*,'[1] the ubiquitous and of- ten ancient corncribs that dot the Galician landscape.

Galician culture is essentially agrarian which, José pointed out, is very hard work. He said that all households with even the tiniest plot of land would grow a patch of corn. Corn bread and a soup made with corn are staples of the farm diet. Corn also feeds the dairy cows. Galicia is a major supplier of milk and cheese, so preserving the corn harvest is crucial.

The hórreos are built on stone stilts that serve two purposes. They keep the harvested corn up above any flooding in the rainy, river-rich province, and the shape of the capstones on stilts prevents rodents from getting to the grain. The sides of the hórreos are slotted to allow for ventilation, which prevents mildew in the damp weather. All of this, José communicated with slow, careful Spanish and hand gestures.

He drove us to a church dating from 1327 and showed us the ancient gravestones on which no names appear. Instead, symbols indicating the occupation of the deceased are carved into the ancient stone slabs. Footprints indicate a *zapatero* (shoe maker), an anchor in a circle indicates a sailor/boatman, and line drawings of the tools of the trade indicate carpenters and blacksmiths.

As we arrived in Finisterre, José spotted two peregrinas who were standing at an intersection trying to discern the way. Some pilgrims, rather than stopping their walk in Santiago, continue on foot to Finisterre—literally translated as 'the end of the earth'—where it is said that the pagans used to gather to worship the setting of the sun. José rolled down the car windows to shout,"Buen Camino!" and point the way for them.

He told them that his passengers (me and Dad) were also pilgrims. We asked the two women where they had begun their pilgrimages. One had started in León. The other, a young woman, had started in Switzerland. She had already walked 2000 kilometers and soon would reach the end of the earth. We congratulated them both and went on our way.

As we approached the shoreline, we passed another pilgrim family, a mother and her young daughter (about eight or nine years old) leading a burro loaded with packs, a toddler brother seated on top, followed by Dad leading a second burro, also bearing packs and an even younger child. They were carrying flowers and leaning into the wind that whips the coast.

We slowly drove onward and upward until, finally, José parked the car. We got out and he pointed the way for us to walk out to the edge. Dad and I walked on and were soon greeted by familiar faces, pilgrims we had met along the way. Some we had not seen for weeks, others we had seen the day before in Santiago.

At the very edge, there is a stone cross where some pilgrims leave tokens. There is also a fire pit where many pilgrims burn something they have carried or used on the journey. Some burn clothes. Some even burn their boots. Tending the fire was our friend Tina whom we had first met in Lorca and whose presence was one of the joyous constants of our trek.

Dad and I consigned nothing to the flames, but stood in the whipping wind and billowing smoke, and looked out beyond the edge of the earth. This was once the very last bit of the known world. What lay beyond the ocean's horizon was as much a matter of speculation and faith as what lies beyond death.

I took Dustin's ashes out of the pouch around my neck and set the little container at the base of the cross, pausing there before taking it up again. I scrambled out onto the rocks beyond the fire pit, carefully opened the canister, and flung the ashes up into the wind. As the wind caught the ashes, Tina began to sing in a beautiful, clear soprano—*Amazing Grace*. An ethereal sound, carried with Dusty's ashes on the wind, singing his flight at Land's End.

I bent down and scooped some bits of sand and stone from the edge of the earth into the tiny canister. I would carry this home to Dustin's mother to put in her garden of remembrance at home. After a tearful embrace with Tina, we all bowed our heads for a moment, then Dad and I turned back to the known world and a smiling José.

From Finisterre it is a short drive to Muxia, an even smaller village and another edge place. Again, we scrambled out on the rocks to see the ocean waves breaking huge and turquoise blue under a glowing gray autumnal sky. Deep breaths, and back to the taxi for the return trip into Santiago. We had done all that we set out to do. Now we would make our way home.

---

## Harold's Journal

Day 47. October 22, 2012

Up at 8:00. This is the last day before we start to travel home. Tomorrow we go to Madrid. The next day we go home. Today we get ready. Souvenir shopping is done. Warm weather with intermittent rain. Ran into Carol and had dinner with her.

Day 48. October 23, 2012

Up at 8:00. Packed and ready to travel by 9:15. Nothing to do until the train leaves for Madrid at 4:05 this afternoon. Train to Madrid left on time. Arrived Madrid at 9:48. Took taxi to our hotel near the airport. In bed about 11:00.

Day 49. October 24, 2012

Up at 6:00. Took the shuttle to the airport at 7:00. Arrived at the airport at 7:30. British Airways flight to London more than 2 hours late. Was switched to Iberia flying into Chicago and then to Houston via American Airline flight 3880. Iberia left Spain on time and arrived Chicago a few minutes early.[2]

---

# Notes

[1] "Hórreo." - *Wikipedia, the Free Encyclopedia.* Web. 06 Oct. 2013. http://en.m.wikipedia.org/wiki/Hórreo

[2] While we were in Santiago, Dad and I bought inexpensive satchels at a little luggage store that were just right for carrying our packs back through the baggage handling gauntlet on the trip home.

# CHAPTER 20

# Returning Home, Still On Camino

---

## *Linda's Journal*

*October 28 –*

*I arrived home last night about 8 PM. At last. The sound of 'my' ocean, the cool Pacific air, the full moon and a full house (the Giants are in the World Series and Travis' pals were all here in the den to watch the game on the big-screen TV). I have a full week before I'm 'supposed to be' back at work, and I'm hoping I take the time to allow a settling, sifting, and integration.*

*I find myself pausing to savor the environment that is home—my habitat—office, kitchen, bedroom, bathrooms, living room, all the luxuries and comforts, all the familiarities.*

*October 29 –*

*Still adjusting to the time change—with daylight savings time due to end soon, I guess this is a 'good' time to be dealing with jet lag. Am slowly beginning to reacquaint myself with my office, closet, where things belong, where to find things. It is Monday and the challenge to stay 'on vacation' begins in earnest today. I find myself seeking a 'program' for improved health—mental, physical, spiritual— anything would (apparently) be preferable to sitting, walking, bik- ing, or driving with nothing but my own thoughts and emotions for company. Maybe today I will go through the bedroom closet and shelves and clear out stuff.*

---

The first thing I noticed on arriving home was my new re- lationship with shoes. It no longer mattered how cute a pair was, if it pinched my toes, it was banished. Shoes were not the only things flying out the door. The Camino is a minimalist experience. After making do with so little, the amount of *stuff* in my closets, cabinets, drawers and on shelves, tables and floor was suffocating. Someone at Goodwill scored BIG that November. It also became apparent that my impatience with clutter extended beyond the physical.

Before the Camino, I often felt like I was nothing more than a Big Head, sitting in a chair, staring at a screen and thinking—*living*—a virtual life. I'd anticipated having lots of time on the Camino to consider the nagging questions that haunt the borders of my life—"first world problem" questions about the meaning, value, and appropriateness of my career choices, questions about what to do with my remaining days.

I did not ponder the deep questions. My thoughts were wholly taken up with the immediate moment—how many more steps I could take before I had to sit down, should I pee behind *this* bush, or maybe *that* one, how long since the last meal and how long 'til the next, what was the weather doing or about to do...

It was an experience of re-embodiment. The immediacy and constancy of the physical imperatives as I walked—

monitoring my body, my surroundings, what I'd eat, where I'd sleep, the number and weight of the possessions I carried, and engaging other people in a foreign land and language—caused me to shift from experience comprehended through thought, to direct experience.

On the Camino, every moment is grasped and engaged through full-spectrum sensory perception. Without consciously observing or 'figuring it out,' I would know, from the way the air felt on my skin, that it was time to stop, put down the packs and put on our rain gear. I'd tell Dad, "It's about to rain. Let's get on our gear." We'd stop. And a few *seconds* after we'd hefted our packs back up and started walking again the rain would begin to fall. I called it "being the full creature."

Having lived as that full-sensory creature for two months, coming back into my office-life was disconcerting. The office felt small. The computer screen sucked all the air from the room. Hovering in the background, like puppets waiting to be reanimated, were all the "Presentation Personae" through which I'd inhabited my 'normal' life. There was the persona my clients expected to see, the one I carefully presented to family, to friends, to colleagues, and neighbors. These scrapbook versions of 'me' were strewn across every space in my life, cluttering the surfaces, blocking the path. The dissonance between the simple 'me' that walked the Camino and the intricately constructed 'me' that had accreted over the course of my adulthood disorganized my habitudes.

I couldn't sit at the desk for more than a few minutes. I couldn't want to do my work. I moved all the office furniture around, placing the computer in a small corner and dragging the easel and paints in from the garage. I left a large space clear in the center of the room—in case I felt like dancing.

When I came down to the office in the morning, where before I'd checked the schedule and to-do list and started cranking out billable hours, I now would sit and wait. Like the creature sensing for rain, I'd sense what 'wanted' to be done. Was I going to answer email? Was I going to prepare a draft contract? Was I going to paint? Dance? Just sit still?

Try as I might, I could not make myself approach the tasks in any other way. Choices were no longer governed by deadlines or priorities imposed by conventional perspectives. Decisions about what to do and when were now made by asking myself, "Does Life come from it?" It was extremely worrying.

I worried that I'd flake out completely, miss deadlines, fail to complete work, lose my clients, tank my career and destroy my family's financial well-being. But that hasn't happened.

One year later, I'm still struggling with the dissonance and disorganization. It is not a comfortable thing to live by this sort of sensing—what Tama J. Kieves calls "fierce guidance," but it is the only option for me anymore. My practice is flourishing. I've continued to earn a fine living, and I've even written this book and am well into the writing of another. I paint more often than I ever have before. And sometimes, when the legal work gets heavy or turbulent, I get up from my desk, put a song with driving rhythms on the player, crank up the volume, and dance.

# Camino Reflections
## (Harold's Afterword)

August 18, 2013

A year ago I was busily preparing for my pilgrimage with my daughter, Linda Alvarez, on the Camino de Santiago. At 82 years old, my major concern was whether I would be strong enough to make a 500-mile hike through the mountains and plains of Spain. I had started walking in February right after finding the movie *The Way* in my mailbox and making the decision to do the pilgrimage. I kept a spreadsheet of my daily hikes as I built up from three miles per day to about seven miles per day. About two months before leaving, I bought my backpack (an Osprey 44), and filled it with all the stuff I planned to carry on the Camino. The total weight came to about twenty pounds not counting water and food. By the last day of preparation, I had hiked a total of exactly 1,000 miles. The last 530 miles of preparation were hiked in the boots (Lowa Renegades) I planned to wear on the Camino. I still left not sure that I was prepared.

I made the pilgrimage with no physical problems other than terribly sore feet at the end of each day.

Linda is one of the easiest people in the world to spend extended time with. Since we have been taking hiking vacations together every two or three years, we had some history of how to accommodate each other. I tend to walk faster than she. Knowing this, I always walked behind her and let her set the pace. I don't mind walking slower and it reduced the stress for her.

For me, it was a blessed time from beginning to end.

I had no idea how I would feel about the pilgrimage after returning home and having time to reflect on the experience. In some book I read about the Camino, the author said, "The Camino doesn't start until you return home." That was certainly true for me.

On the Camino we met many interesting and wonderful people. There were very few pilgrims who were difficult in any way. Part of this is true since all are "united against a common foe"—the Camino itself. The major part, however, was that everyone was completely equal. Neither a person's nationality, age, gender, race, economic status or anything else mattered. We all discovered that we can live life without all of that "stuff." Everything we owned was in our backpack or our pockets. Whenever a need arose, no matter what, all of our fellow pilgrims immediately came to our rescue.

On returning home, I had no idea how much the Camino experience would dominate my thinking. I think about the Camino and the lessons I learned every day. No matter what happens in my daily life I find that somehow I relate my new experience to something I learned on the Camino. I think about the people I met and the lessons I learned from their response to hardship. I think about the gracious acceptance of the pilgrims and of the Spanish business people and residents along the Camino. I am blessed by the increased bonding and appreciation I feel for my daughter.

I am blessed to be home and with my wife and neighbors. I have no interest in doing the Camino again but I think it is one of the most significant and rewarding experiences of my life.

## FINIS

100

34317096R00121

Made in the USA
Lexington, KY
02 August 2014